FIX-IT and FORGET-IT®
Lighter
Quick & Easy Recipes

Fix-It and FORGET-It®
Lighter
Quick & Easy Recipes

Healthy Instant Pot®
& Slow Cooker Meals

127
Lower Calorie
& Delicious
Dishes

HOPE COMERFORD
PHOTOGRAPHS BY BONNIE MATTHEWS

Good Books

New York, New York

Good Books books may be purchased in bulk at special discounts for sales promotion, corporate gifts, fund-raising, or educational purposes. Special editions can also be created to specifications. For details, contact the Special Sales Department, Good Books, 307 West 36th Street, 11th Floor, New York, NY 10018 or info@skyhorsepublishing.com.

Good Books is an imprint of Skyhorse Publishing, Inc.®, a Delaware corporation.

Visit our website at www.goodbooks.com.

10 9 8 7 6 5 4 3 2 1

Library of Congress Cataloging-in-Publication Data

Names: Comerford, Hope, author. | Matthews, Bonnie, 1963- photographer.
Title: Fix-it and forget-it lighter quick & easy recipes : healthy instant
   pot & slow cooker meals : 127 lower calorie & delicious dishes / Hope
   Comerford ; photographs by Bonnie Matthews.
Other titles: Fix it and forget it lighter quick and easy recipes
Description: New York, New York : Good Books, [2024] | Series: Fix-it and
   forget-it | Includes index. | Summary: "127 Instant Pot and slow cooker
   meals for a healthier, lighter you"-- Provided by publisher.
Identifiers: LCCN 2023050824 (print) | LCCN 2023050825 (ebook) | ISBN
   9781680999150 (paperback) | ISBN 9781680999280 (epub)
Subjects: LCSH: Electric cooking, Slow. | Quick and easy cooking. |
   One-dish meals. | Low-fat diet--Recipes. | LCGFT: Cookbooks.
Classification: LCC TX827 .C639 2024 (print) | LCC TX827 (ebook) | DDC
   641.5/884--dc23/eng/20231204
LC record available at https://lccn.loc.gov/2023050824
LC ebook record available at https://lccn.loc.gov/2023050825

Cover design by Kai Texel
Cover photo by Bonnie Matthews

Print ISBN: 978-1-68099-915-0
Ebook ISBN: 978-1-68099-928-0

Printed in China

Contents

Welcome to *Fix-It and Forget-It Lighter Quick & Easy* ⚜ 1

Choosing a Slow Cooker ⚜ 1

Get to Know Your Slow Cooker ⚜ 3

Slow Cooker Tips, Tricks & Other Things You May Not Know ⚜ 5

What Is an Instant Pot? ⚜ 6

Getting Started with Your Instant Pot ⚜ 8

Instant Pot Tips, Tricks & Other Things You May Not Know ⚜ 10

Instant Pot Accessories ⚜ 13

⚜ Recipes ⚜

Appetizers & Snacks ⚜ 15

Breakfasts ⚜ 27

Soups, Stews & Chilis ⚜ 43

Main Dishes ⚜ 71

Chicken & Turkey ⚜ 73

Pork ⚜ 101

Beef ⚜ 113

Meatless ⚜ 127

Seafood ⚜ 143

Side Dishes ⚜ 155

Desserts ⚜ 185

Metric Equivalent Measurements ⚜ 205

Recipe & Ingredient Index ⚜ 206

About the Author ⚜ 217

Welcome to Fix-It and Forget-It Lighter Quick & Easy!

As busy as life is, having some go-to "quick & easy" recipes is a must! In this book, you'll find 127 recipes, all for a slow cooker or Instant Pot. The recipes included in this book are easy to assemble, and cook in a reasonable amount of time! As an added bonus, I've made sure they're a bit "lighter" for you as well. As always, please make substitutions to ingredients as you see fit. "Lighter" can mean different things for different people. Nutrition info is included for all recipes in this book, but of course that information will no longer be accurate if you alter the ingredients.

Choosing a Slow Cooker

Not all slow cookers are created equal . . . or work equally as well for everyone!

Those of us who use slow cookers frequently know we have our own preferences when it comes to which slow cooker we choose to use. For instance, I love my programmable slow cooker, but there are many programmable slow cookers I've tried that I've strongly disliked. Why? Because some go by increments of 15 or 30 minutes and some go by 4, 6, 8, or 10 hours. I dislike those restrictions, but I have family and friends who don't mind them at all! I am also pretty brand loyal when it comes to my manual slow cookers because I've had great success with those and have had unsuccessful moments with slow cookers of other brands. So, which slow cooker(s) is/are best for your household?

It really depends on how many people you're feeding and if you're gone for long periods of time. Here are my recommendations:

For 2–3 person household	3–5 quart slow cooker
For 4–5 person household	5–6 quart slow cooker
For 6+ person household	6½–7 quart slow cooker

Large slow cooker advantages/disadvantages:

Advantages:
- You can fit a loaf pan or a baking dish into a 6- or 7-quart, depending on the shape of your cooker. That allows you to make bread or cakes, or even smaller quantities of main dishes. (Take your favorite baking dish and loaf pan along when you shop for a cooker to make sure they'll fit inside.)
- You can feed large groups of people, or make larger quantities of food, allowing for leftovers, or meals, to freeze.

Disadvantages:
- They take up more storage room.
- They don't fit as neatly into a dishwasher.
- If your crock isn't ⅔–¾ full, you may burn your food.

Small slow cooker advantages/disadvantages:

Advantages:
- They're great for lots of appetizers, for serving hot drinks, for baking cakes straight in the crock, and for dorm rooms or apartments.
- Great option for making recipes of smaller quantities.

Disadvantages:
- Food in smaller quantities tends to cook more quickly than larger amounts. So keep an eye on it.
- Chances are, you won't have many leftovers. So, if you like to have leftovers, a smaller slow cooker may not be a good option for you.

My Recommendation

Have at least two slow cookers: one around 3 to 4 quarts and one 6 quarts or larger. A third would be a huge bonus (and a great advantage to your cooking repertoire!). The advantage of having at least a couple is you can make a larger variety of recipes. Also, you can make at least two or three dishes at once for a whole meal.

Manual vs. Programmable

If you are gone for only six to eight hours a day, a manual slow cooker might be just fine for you. If you are gone for more than eight hours during the day, I would highly recommend purchasing a programmable slow cooker that will switch to warm when the cook time you set is up. It will allow you to cook a wider variety of recipes.

The two I use most frequently are my 4-quart manual slow cooker and my 6½-quart programmable slow cooker. I like that I can make smaller portions in my 4-quart slow cooker on days I don't need or want leftovers, but I also love how my 6½-quart slow cooker can accommodate whole chickens, turkey breasts, hams, or big batches of soups. I use them both often.

Get to Know Your Slow Cooker

Plan a little time to get acquainted with your slow cooker. Each slow cooker has its own personality—just like your oven (and your car). Plus, many new slow cookers cook hotter and faster than earlier models. I think that with all of the concern for food safety, the slow-cooker manufacturers have amped up their settings so that "High," "Low," and "Warm" are all higher temperatures than in the older models. That means they cook hotter—and therefore, faster—than the first slow cookers. The beauty of these little machines is that they're supposed to cook low and slow. We count on that when we flip the switch in the morning before we leave the house for ten hours or so. So, because none of us knows what kind of temperament our slow cooker has until we try it out, nor how hot it cooks—don't assume anything. Save yourself a disappointment and make the first recipe in your new slow cooker on a day when you're at home. Cook it for the shortest amount of time the recipe calls for. Then, check the food to see if it's done. Or if you start smelling food that seems to be finished, turn off the cooker and rescue your food.

Also, all slow cookers seem to have a "hot spot," which is of great importance to know, especially when baking with your slow cooker. This spot may tend to burn food in that area if you're not careful. If you're baking directly in your slow cooker, I recommend covering the "hot spot" with some foil.

Take Notes

Don't be afraid to make notes in your cookbook. It's yours! Chances are, it will eventually get passed down to someone in your family and they will love and appreciate all of your musings. Take note of which slow cooker you used and exactly how long it took to cook the recipe. The next time you make it, you won't need to try to remember. Apply what you learned to the next recipes you make in your cooker. If another recipe says it needs to cook 7–9 hours, and you've discovered your slow cooker cooks on the faster side, cook that recipe for 6–6½ hours and then check it. You can always cook a recipe longer—but you can't reverse things if it's overdone.

Get creative . . .

If you know your morning is going to be hectic, prepare everything the night before, take it out so the crock warms up to room temperature when you first get up in the morning, then plug it in and turn it on as you're leaving the house.

If you want to make something that has a short cook time and you're going to be gone longer than that, cook it the night before and refrigerate it for the next day. Warm it up when you get home. Or, cook those recipes on the weekend when you know you'll be home and eat them later in the week.

Slow Cooker Tips, Tricks & Other Things You May Not Know

- Slow cookers tend to work best when they're ⅔ to ¾ of the way full. You may need to increase the cooking time if you've exceeded that amount, or reduce it if you've put in less than that. If you're going to exceed that limit, it would be best to reduce the recipe, or split it between two slow cookers. (Remember how I suggested owning at least two or three slow cookers?)

- Keep your veggies on the bottom. That puts them in more direct contact with the heat. The fuller your slow cooker, the longer it will take its contents to cook. Also, the more densely packed the cooker's contents are, the longer they will take to cook. And finally, the larger the chunks of meat or vegetables, the more time they will need to cook.

- Keep the lid on! Every time you take a peek, you lose 20 minutes of cooking time. Please take this into consideration each time you lift the lid! I know, some of you can't help yourself and are going to lift anyway. Just don't forget to tack on 20 minutes to your cook time for each time you peeked!

- Sometimes it's beneficial to remove the lid. If you'd like your dish to thicken a bit, take the lid off during the last half hour to hour of cooking time.

- If you have a big slow cooker (7- to 8-quart), you can cook a small batch in it by putting the recipe ingredients into an oven-safe baking dish or baking pan and then placing that into the cooker's crock. First, put a trivet or some metal jar rings on the bottom of the crock, and then set your dish or pan on top of them. Or a loaf pan may "hook onto" the top ridges of the crock belonging to a large oval cooker and hang there straight and securely, "baking" a cake or quick bread. Cover the cooker and flip it on.

- The outside of your slow cooker will be hot! Please remember to keep it out of reach of children and keep that in mind for yourself as well!

- Get yourself a quick-read meat thermometer and use it! This helps remove the question of whether or not your meat is fully cooked, and helps prevent you from overcooking your meat as well.
    - Internal Cooking Temperatures: Beef—125–130°F (rare); 140–145°F (medium); 160°F (well-done)
    - Pork—140–145°F (rare); 145–150°F (medium); 160°F (well-done)
    - Turkey and Chicken—165°F
    - Frozen meat: The basic rule of thumb is, don't put frozen meat into the slow cooker. The meat does not reach the proper internal temperature in time. This especially applies to thick cuts of meat! Proceed with caution!
- Add fresh herbs 10 minutes before the end of the cooking time to maximize their flavor.
- If your recipe calls for cooked pasta, add it 10 minutes before the end of the cooking time if the cooker is on High; 30 minutes before the end of the cooking time if it's on Low. Then the pasta won't get mushy.
- If your recipe calls for sour cream or cream, stir it in 5 minutes before the end of the cooking time. You want it to heat but not boil or simmer.
    - Approximate Slow Cooker Temperatures (Remember, each slow cooker is different): High—212°F–300°F
    - Low—170°F–200°F
    - Simmer—185°F
    - Warm—165°F
- Cooked beans freeze well. Store them in freezer bags (squeeze the air out first) or freezer boxes. Cooked and dried bean measurements:16-oz. can, drained = about 1¾ cups beans
    - 19-oz. can, drained = about 2 cups beans
    - 1 lb. dried beans (about 2½ cups) = 5 cups cooked beans

What Is an Instant Pot?

In short, an Instant Pot is a digital pressure cooker that also has multiple other functions. Not only can it be used as a pressure cooker, but depending on which model Instant Pot you have, you can set it to do things like sauté, cook rice, grains, porridge, soup/stew, beans/chili, porridge, meat, poultry, cake, and eggs, and make yogurt. You can use the Instant Pot to steam or slow cook or even set it manually. Because the Instant Pot has so many functions, it takes away the need for multiple appliances on your counter and allows you to use fewer pots and pans.

Getting Started with Your Instant Pot

Get to Know Your Instant Pot . . .

The very first thing most Instant Pot owners do is called the water test. It helps you get to know your Instant Pot a bit, familiarizes you with it, and might even take a bit of your apprehension away (because if you're anything like me, I was scared to death to use it).

Step 1: Plug in your Instant Pot. This may seem obvious to some, but when we're nervous about using a new appliance, sometimes we forget things like this.

Step 2: Make sure the inner pot is inserted in the cooker. You should *never* attempt to cook anything in your device without the inner pot, or you will ruin your Instant Pot. Food should never come into contact with the actual housing unit.

Step 3: The inner pot has lines for each cup. Fill the inner pot with water until it reaches the 3-cup line.

Step 4: Check the sealing ring to be sure it's secure and in place. You should not be able to move it around. If it's not in place properly, you may experience issues with the pot letting out a lot of steam while cooking, or not coming to pressure.

Step 5: Seal the lid. There is an arrow on the lid between "open" and "close." There is also an arrow on the top of the base of the Instant Pot between a picture of a locked lock and an unlocked lock. Line those arrows up, then turn the lid toward the picture of the lock (left). You will hear a noise that will indicate the lid is locked. If you do not hear a noise, it's not locked. Try it again.

Step 6: *Always* check to see if the steam valve on top of the lid is turned to "sealing." If it's not on "sealing" and is on "venting," it will not be able to come to pressure.

Step 7: Press the "Steam" button and use the +/- arrow to set it to 2 minutes. Once it's at the desired time, you don't need to press anything else. In a few seconds, the Instant Pot will begin all on its own. For those of us with digital slow cookers, we have a tendency to look for the "start" button, but there isn't one on the Instant Pot.

Step 8: Now you wait for the "magic" to happen! The cooking will begin once the device comes to pressure. This can take anywhere from 5 to 30 minutes, in my experience. Then, you will see the countdown happen (from the time you set it for). After that, the Instant Pot will beep, which means your meal is done!

Step 9: Your Instant Pot will now automatically switch to "warm" and begin a count of how many minutes it's been on warm. The next part is where you either wait for the NPR, or natural pressure release (the pressure releases on its own), or do what's called a QR, or quick release (you manually release the pressure). Which method you choose depends on what you're cooking, but in this case, you can choose either, because it's just water. For NPR, you will wait for the lever to move all the way back over to "venting" and watch the pinion (float valve) next to the lever. It will be flush with the lid when at full pressure and will drop when the pressure is done releasing. If you choose QR, be very careful not to have your hands over the vent, as the steam is very hot and you can burn yourself.

The Three Most Important Buttons You Need to Know About

You will find the majority of recipes will use the following three buttons:

Manual/Pressure Cook: Some older models tend to say "Manual," and the newer models seem to say "Pressure Cook." They mean the same thing. From here, you use the +/- button to change the cook time. After several seconds, the Instant Pot will begin its process. The exact name of this button will vary on your model of Instant Pot.

Sauté: Many recipes will have you sauté vegetables, or brown meat before beginning the pressure cooking process. For this setting, you will not use the lid of the Instant Pot.

Keep Warm/Cancel: This may just be the most important button on the Instant Pot. When you forget to use the +/- buttons to change the time for a recipe, or you press a wrong button, you can hit "Keep Warm/Cancel" and it will turn your Instant Pot off for you.

What Do All the Buttons Do?

With so many buttons, it's hard to remember what each one does or means. You can use this as a quick guide in a pinch.

Soup/Broth. This button cooks at high pressure for 30 minutes. It can be adjusted using the +/- buttons to cook more, for 40 minutes, or less, for 20 minutes.

Meat/Stew. This button cooks at high pressure for 35 minutes. It can be adjusted using the +/- buttons to cook more, for 45 minutes, or less, for 20 minutes.

Bean/Chili. This button cooks at high pressure for 30 minutes. It can be adjusted using the +/- buttons to cook more, for 40 minutes, or less, for 25 minutes.

Poultry. This button cooks at high pressure for 15 minutes. It can be adjusted using the +/- buttons to cook more, for 30 minutes, or less, for 5 minutes.

Rice. This button cooks at low pressure and is the only fully automatic program. It is for cooking white rice and will automatically adjust the cooking time depending on the amount of water and rice in the cooking pot.

Multigrain. This button cooks at high pressure for 40 minutes. It can be adjusted using the +/- buttons to cook more, for 45 minutes of warm water soaking time and 60 minutes pressure cooking time, or less, for 20 minutes.

Porridge. This button cooks at high pressure for 20 minutes. It can be adjusted using the +/- buttons to cook more, for 30 minutes, or less, for 15 minutes.

Steam. This button cooks at high pressure for 10 minutes. It can be adjusted using the +/- buttons to cook more, for 15 minutes, or less, for 3 minutes. Always use a rack or steamer basket with this function, because it heats at full power continuously while it's coming to pressure, and you do not want food in direct contact with the bottom of the pressure cooking pot or it will burn. Once it reaches pressure, the steam button regulates pressure by cycling on and off, similar to the other pressure buttons.

Less | Normal | More. Adjust between the *Less | Normal | More* settings by pressing the same cooking function button repeatedly until you get to the desired setting. (Older versions use the *Adjust* button.)

+/- Buttons. Adjust the cook time up [+] or down [-]. (On newer models, you can also press and hold [-] or [+] for 3 seconds to turn sound OFF or ON.)

Cake. This button cooks at high pressure for 30 minutes. It can be adjusted using the +/- buttons to cook more, for 40 minutes, or less, for 25 minutes.

Egg. This button cooks at high pressure for 5 minutes. It can be adjusted using the +/- buttons to cook more, for 6 minutes, or less, for 4 minutes.

Instant Pot Tips, Tricks & Other Things You May Not Know

- Never attempt to cook directly in the Instant Pot without the inner pot!
- Once you set the time, you can walk away. It will show the time you set it to, then will change to the word "on" while the pressure builds. Once the Instant Pot has come to pressure, you will once again see the time you set it for. It will count down from there.
- Always make sure the sealing ring is securely in place. If it shows signs of wear or tear, it needs to be replaced.
- Have a sealing ring for savory recipes and a separate sealing ring for sweet recipes. Many people report their desserts tasting like a roast (or another savory food) if they try to use the same sealing ring for all recipes.
- The stainless steel rack (trivet) the Instant Pot comes with can be used to keep food from being completely submerged in liquid, like baked potatoes or ground beef. It can also be used to set another pot on, for pot-in-pot cooking.

- If you use warm or hot liquid instead of cold liquid, you may need to adjust the cooking time, or the food may not come out done.
- Always double-check to see that the valve on the lid is set to "sealing" and not "venting" when you first lock the lid. This will save you from the Instant Pot not coming to pressure.
- Use Natural Pressure Release for tougher cuts of meat, recipes with high starch (like rice or grains), and recipes with a high volume of liquid. This means you let the Instant Pot naturally release pressure. The little bobbin will fall once pressure is released completely.
- Use Quick Release for more delicate cuts of meat, such as seafood and chicken breasts, and for steaming vegetables. This means you manually turn the vent (being careful not to put your hand over the vent) to release the pressure. The little bobbin will fall once pressure is released completely.
- Make sure there is a clear pathway for the steam to release. The last thing you want is to ruin the bottom of your cupboards with all that steam.
- You *must* use liquid in the Instant Pot. The *minimum* amount of liquid you should have in the inner pot is ½ cup, but most recipes work best with at least 1 cup.
- Do *not* overfill the Instant Pot! It should only be half full for rice or beans (food that expands greatly when cooked) or two-thirds of the way full for almost everything else. Do not fill it to the max fill line.
- In this book, the Cook Time *does not* take into account the amount of time it will take the Instant Pot to come to pressure, or the amount of time it will take the Instant Pot to release pressure. Be aware of this when choosing a recipe to make.
- If the Instant Pot is not coming to pressure, it's usually because the sealing ring is not on properly, or the vent is not set to "sealing."
- The more liquid, or the colder the ingredients, the longer it will take for the Instant Pot to come to pressure.
- Always make sure that the Instant Pot is dry before inserting the inner pot, and make sure the inner pot is dry before inserting it into the Instant Pot.
- Use a binder clip to hold the inner pot tight against the outer pot when sautéing and stirring. This will keep the pot from "spinning" in the base.
- Doubling a recipe does not change the cook time, but instead it will take longer to come up to pressure.
- You do not always need to double the liquid when doubling a recipe. Depending on what you're making, more liquid may make the food too watery. Use your best judgment.
- When using the slow cooker function, use the following chart:

Slow Cooker	Instant Pot
Warm	Less or Low
Low	Normal or Medium
High	More or High

Instant Pot Accessories

Most Instant Pots come with a stainless steel trivet. Below, you will find a list of common accessories that are frequently used in most Fix-It and Forget-It Instant Pot cookbooks. Most of these accessories can be purchased in-store or online.

- Steamer basket—stainless steel or silicone
- 7-inch nonstick or silicone springform or cake pan
- Sling or trivet with handles
- 1½-quart round baking dish
- silicone egg molds

Appetizers & Snacks

Slim Dunk

Vera Schmucker, Goshen, IN

Makes 3 cups, or 12 servings
Prep. Time: 10 minutes   &   Cooking Time: 1 hour   &   Ideal slow-cooker size: 1½-qt.

2 cups fat-free sour cream

¼ cup fat-free Miracle Whip salad dressing

10-oz. pkg. frozen chopped spinach, thawed and squeezed dry

1.8-oz. envelope dry leek soup mix

¼ cup minced red bell pepper

1. Combine all ingredients in slow cooker. Mix well.

2. Cover. Cook on High 1 hour.

3. Serve with fat-free baked tortilla chips.

Calories: 70
Fat: 1g
Sodium: 310mg
Carbs: 11g
Sugar: 0.9g
Protein: 2.5g

Seven Layer Dip

Hope Comerford, Clinton Township, MI

Makes 10–15 servings

Prep. Time: 20 minutes & Cooking Time: 2 hours & Ideal slow-cooker size: 6-qt.

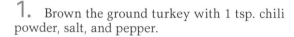

1 lb. lean ground turkey

2½ tsp. chili powder, *divided*

½ tsp. kosher salt

⅛ tsp. pepper

15-oz. can fat-free refried beans

4-oz. can diced green chilies

1 cup nonfat Greek yogurt

1 cup salsa

1 cup shredded Mexican blend cheese

2-oz. can sliced black olives

2 green onions, sliced

1. Brown the ground turkey with 1 tsp. chili powder, salt, and pepper.

2. Meanwhile spray the crock with nonstick spray.

3. Mix together 1 tsp. chili powder with the refried beans, then spread them into a layer at the bottom of the crock.

4. Next add a layer of the diced green chilies.

5. Spread the ground turkey over the top of the green chilies.

6. Mix together the remaining ½ tsp. chili powder with the Greek yogurt, and then spread this over the ground turkey in the crock.

7. Next, spread the salsa over the top.

8. Last, sprinkle the cheese into a layer on top and end with the black olives.

9. Cover and cook on Low for 2 hours. Sprinkle the green onions on top before serving.

Calories: 135
Fat: 6g
Sodium: 420mg
Carbs: 11g
Sugar: 2g
Protein: 12g

Spinach and Artichoke Dip

Michele Ruvola, Vestal, NY

Makes 10–12 servings
Prep. Time: 5 minutes ⚬ *Cooking Time: 4 minutes*

8 oz. low-fat cream cheese

10-oz. box frozen spinach

½ cup no-sodium chicken broth

14-oz. can artichoke hearts, drained

½ cup low-fat sour cream

½ cup low-fat mayonnaise

3 cloves garlic, minced

1 tsp. onion powder

16 oz. shredded reduced-fat Parmesan cheese

1. Put all ingredients in the inner pot of the Instant Pot, except the Parmesan cheese.

2. Secure the lid and set the vent to sealing. Manually set for 4 minutes on high pressure.

3. Manually release the pressure when the cooking time is over.

4. When the pin drops, open the lid and immediately stir in the cheese.

Serving suggestion:
Serve with vegetables or sliced whole-grain bread.

Tip:
This dip will thicken as it cools.

Calories: 244
Fat: 15g
Sodium: 900mg
Carbs: 15g
Sugar: 3g
Protein: 15g

Chicken Lettuce Wraps

SLOW COOKER

Hope Comerford, Clinton Township, MI

Makes about 12 wraps

Prep. Time: 15 minutes   &   Cooking Time: 2–3 hours   &   Ideal slow-cooker size: 5- or 7-qt.

2 lb. ground chicken, browned

4 cloves garlic, minced

½ cup minced sweet yellow onion

4 Tbsp. gluten-free soy sauce or Bragg® liquid aminos

1 Tbsp. natural crunchy peanut butter

1 tsp. rice wine vinegar

1 tsp. sesame oil

¼ tsp. kosher salt

¼ tsp. red pepper flakes

¼ tsp. black pepper

8-oz. can sliced water chestnuts, drained, rinsed, chopped

3 green onions, sliced

12 good-sized pieces of iceberg lettuce, rinsed and patted dry

1. In the crock, combine the ground chicken, garlic, yellow onion, soy sauce or liquid aminos, peanut butter, vinegar, sesame oil, salt, red pepper flakes, and black pepper.

2. Cover and cook on Low for 2–3 hours.

3. Add in the water chestnuts and green onions. Cover and cook for an additional 10–15 minutes.

4. Serve a good spoonful on each piece of iceberg lettuce.

Serving suggestion:
Garnish with diced red bell pepper and diced green onion.

Calories: 135
Fat: 7g
Sodium: 430mg
Carbs: 3.5g
Sugar: 1g
Protein: 14.5g

Gluten-Free Chex Mix

Hope Comerford, Clinton Township, MI

Makes 12 servings
Prep. Time: 8 minutes ⚭ Cooking Time: 3 hours
Cooling Time: 1 hour ⚭ Ideal slow-cooker size: 6- or 7-qt.

3 cups Rice Chex™
3 cups Corn Chex™
3 cups Cheerios™
1 cup unsalted peanuts
⅓ cup coconut oil, melted
4 tsp. gluten-free Worcestershire sauce
1 tsp. sea salt
1 tsp. garlic powder
1 tsp. onion powder

1. Spray the crock with nonstick spray.

2. Place the Rice Chex, Corn Chex, Cheerios, and peanuts in the crock.

3. In a small bowl, whisk together the coconut oil, Worcestershire, sea salt, garlic powder, and onion powder. Pour this over the cereal in the crock and gently mix it with a rubber spatula until all cereal and peanuts are evenly coated.

4. Place a paper towel or thin dishcloth under the lid and cook on low for 3 hours, stirring once at the end of the first hour, once at the end of the second hour, and twice the last hour.

5. Spread the mixture onto parchment paper–lined baking sheets and let them cool for 1 hour.

6. Serve or keep in a sealed container at room temperature for up to 3 weeks.

Calories: 210
Fat: 13g
Sodium: 350mg
Carbs: 21g
Sugar: 3g
Protein: 5g

Cranberry Almond Coconut Snack Mix

SLOW COOKER

Hope Comerford, Clinton Township, MI

Makes 12 servings
Prep. Time: 10 minutes ✤ Cooking Time: 2–3 hours
Cooling Time: 1 hour ✤ Ideal slow-cooker size: 6- or 7-qt.

5 cups Cheerios™
3 cups Honey Nut Cheerios™
1 cup gluten-free oats
1 cup dried cranberries
2 cups unsweetened shredded coconut
2 cups chopped raw almonds
¼ cup melted coconut oil
¼ cup honey
½ tsp. cinnamon
½ tsp. salt
1 tsp. vanilla extract

1. Spray crock with nonstick spray.

2. Place the Cheerios, Honey Nut Cheerios, gluten-free oats, cranberries, coconut, and almonds into the crock.

3. In a bowl, whisk together the coconut oil, honey, cinnamon, salt, and vanilla. Pour this mixture over the cereal in the crock and gently stir with a rubber spatula until everything is evenly coated.

4. Place a paper towel under the lid, cover, and cook on Low for 2–3 hours. Be sure to stir every 45 minutes or so to prevent burning.

5. When done cooking, pour mixture on parchment paper–lined baking sheet and let cool 1 hour. Once cooled, serve or store in an airtight container at room temperature for up to 3 weeks.

Calories: 380
Fat: 23g
Sodium: 200mg
Carbs: 42g
Sugar: 18g
Protein: 8.5g

Insta-Popcorn

Hope Comerford, Clinton Township, MI

Makes 5–6 servings
Prep. Time: 1 minute 🍴 Cooking Time: about 5 minutes

2 Tbsp. coconut oil

½ cup popcorn kernels

¼ cup margarine spread, melted, *optional*

Sea salt to taste

1. Set the Instant Pot to Sauté.

2. Melt the coconut oil in the inner pot, then add the popcorn kernels and stir.

3. Press Adjust to bring the temperature up to high.

4. When the corn starts popping, secure the lid on the Instant Pot.

5. When you no longer hear popping, turn off the Instant Pot, remove the lid, and carefully pour the popcorn into a bowl.

6. Top with the optional melted margarine and season the popcorn with sea salt to your liking.

Calories: 161
Fat: 13g
Sodium: 89mg
Carbs: 13g
Sugar: 0g
Protein: 2g

Breakfasts

Giant Healthy Pancake

Hope Comerford, Clinton Township, MI

Makes 4 servings
Prep. Time: 10 minutes ♣ Cooking Time: 17 minutes

¾ cup whole wheat flour

¼ cup all-purpose flour

¾ tsp. baking powder

¾ tsp. baking soda

1 large egg

1¼ cups unsweetened almond milk

1½ Tbsp. unsweetened applesauce

1 cup water

Serving suggestion:

Serve with maple syrup, a drizzle of honey, or topped with your favorite fruit.

1. In a bowl, mix the whole wheat flour, all-purpose flour, baking powder, and baking soda.

2. In a smaller bowl, mix the egg, milk, and unsweetened applesauce until well combined. Pour into the dry ingredients and stir until well combined.

3. Spray a 7-inch round springform pan with nonstick cooking spray and then pour the pancake batter into it.

4. Pour the water into the inner pot of the Instant Pot. Place the springform pan on the trivet and carefully lower the trivet into the inner pot.

5. Secure the lid and make sure the vent is set to sealing.

6. Manually set your Instant Pot to Low pressure and set the cook time for 17 minutes.

7. When the cook time is over, manually release the pressure.

8. Remove the lid and carefully lift the trivet out with oven mitts.

9. Remove the cake from the pan and allow to cool for a few minutes before serving and to allow the moisture on the surface of the cake to dry.

Calories: 173
Fat: 2.8g
Sodium: 475mg
Carbs: 33g
Sugar: 9g
Protein: 6g

SLOW COOKER

Fiesta Hashbrowns

Dena Mell-Dorchy, Royal Oak, MI

Makes 8 servings
Prep. Time: 15 minutes ❧ Cooking Time: 8–9 hours ❧ Ideal slow-cooker size: 3- or 4-qt.

1 lb. ground turkey sausage

½ cup chopped onion

5 cups gluten-free frozen diced hash browns

8 oz. gluten-free low-sodium chicken stock

1 small red sweet pepper

1 jalapeño, seeded and finely diced

1½ cups sliced mushrooms

2 Tbsp. quick-cooking tapioca

½ cup shredded Monterey Jack cheese

1. Spray slow cooker with nonstick spray.

2. In a large skillet, brown sausage and onion over medium heat. Drain off fat.

3. Combine sausage mixture, hash browns, chicken stock, sweet pepper, jalapeño, mushrooms, and tapioca in cooker; stir to combine.

4. Cover and cook on Low heat for 8–9 hours. Stir before serving. Top with shredded Monterey Jack cheese.

Calories: 275
Fat: 10g
Sodium: 500mg
Carbs: 29g
Sugar: 2g
Protein: 18g

Vegetarian Sausage and Sweet Pepper Hash

Hope Comerford Clinton Township, MI

Makes 6–8 servings

Prep. Time: 10 minutes ⚬ *Cooking Time: 6½ hours* ⚬ *Ideal slow-cooker size: 4-qt.*

14-oz. package vegetarian Italian sausage, cut lengthwise, then into ½-inch pieces

16 oz. frozen diced potatoes

1½ cups sliced onion

3 bell peppers, sliced (color of your choice)

¼ cup olive oil

1 tsp. sea salt

½ tsp. pepper

½ tsp. dried thyme

½ tsp. dried parsley

½ cup nutritional yeast

1. Spray crock with vegan nonstick spray.

2. Place sausage, frozen potatoes, onion, and sliced peppers into crock.

3. Mix with the olive oil, salt, pepper, thyme, parsley, and nutritional yeast.

4. Cover and cook on Low for 6 hours.

Calories: 263
Fat: 16g
Sodium: 658mg
Carbs: 19g
Sugar: 3g
Protein: 14g

Breakfast Sausage Casserole

SLOW COOKER

Kendra Dreps, Liberty, PA

Makes 8 servings
Prep. Time: 15 minutes ❧ Chilling Time: 8 hours
Cooking Time: 4 hours ❧ Ideal slow-cooker size: 3-qt.

1 lb. meatless sausage crumbles

6 eggs

2 cups nondairy milk

8 slices whole-grain or sprouted-grain bread, cubed

1 cup reduced-fat shredded cheddar cheese

1. In a nonstick skillet, brown and drain sausage.

2. Mix eggs and milk in a large bowl.

3. Stir in bread cubes, cheese, and sausage.

4. Place in greased slow cooker.

5. Refrigerate overnight.

6. Cook on Low for 4 hours.

Variation:

Use cubed cooked ham instead of sausage.

Calories: 358
Fat: 22.2g
Sodium: 861mg
Carbs: 16g
Sugar: 1g
Protein: 27g

SLOW
COOKER

Spinach Frittata

Shirley Unternahrer, Wayland, IA

Makes 4–6 servings
Prep. Time: 15 minutes   ☙   Cooking Time: 1½–2 hours   ☙   Ideal slow-cooker size: 5-qt.

4 eggs

½ tsp. kosher salt

½ tsp. dried basil

Fresh ground pepper to taste

3 cups chopped fresh spinach, stems removed

½ cup chopped tomato, liquid drained off

⅓ cup freshly grated Parmesan cheese

1. Whisk eggs well in mixing bowl. Whisk in salt, basil, and pepper.

2. Gently stir in spinach, tomato, and Parmesan.

3. Pour into lightly greased slow cooker.

4. Cover and cook on High for 1½–2 hours, until middle is set. Serve hot.

Calories: 90
Fat: 5.5g
Sodium: 420mg
Carbs: 3g
Sugar: .5g
Protein: 7g

Italian Frittata

SLOW COOKER

Hope Comerford, Clinton Township, MI

Makes 6 servings
Prep. Time: 10 minutes & Cooking Time: 3–4 hours & Ideal slow-cooker size: 5- or 6-qt.

10 eggs
1 Tbsp. chopped fresh basil
1 Tbsp. chopped fresh mint
1 Tbsp. chopped fresh sage
1 Tbsp. chopped fresh oregano
½ tsp. sea salt
⅛ tsp. pepper
1 Tbsp. grated Parmesan cheese
¼ cup diced prosciutto
½ cup chopped onion

1. Spray your crock with nonstick spray.

2. In a bowl, mix the eggs, basil, mint, sage, oregano, sea salt, pepper, and Parmesan. Pour this mixture into the crock.

3. Sprinkle the prosciutto and onion evenly over the egg mixture in the crock.

4. Cover and cook on Low for 3–4 hours.

Calories: 145
Fat: 9g
Sodium: 370mg
Carbs: 2.5g
Sugar: 1g
Protein: 12.5g

Pumpkin Breakfast Custard

Audrey Hess, Gettysburg, PA

Makes 4–6 servings

Prep. Time: 20 minutes   ❧   Cooking Time: 1½–2 hours   ❧   Ideal slow-cooker size: 2½- or 3-qt.

2½ cups cooked, peeled, and pureed or canned pumpkin or winter squash

2 Tbsp. blackstrap molasses

3 Tbsp. maple syrup

¼ cup half-and-half

3 eggs

1 tsp. cinnamon

½ tsp. ground ginger

½ tsp. ground nutmeg

¼ tsp. ground cloves

¼ tsp. salt

1. Puree ingredients in blender until smooth.

2. Pour into greased slow cooker.

3. Cook on High for 1½–2 hours, until set in the middle and just browning at edges.

4. Serve warm in scoops over hot cereal, baked oatmeal, or as a breakfast side dish with toast or muffins.

Calories: 150
Fat: 4.5g
Sodium: 170mg
Carbs: 26g
Sugar: 14g
Protein: 4.5g

Best Steel-Cut Oats

Colleen Heatwole, Burton, MI

Makes 4 servings
Prep. Time: 5 minutes ⚖ Cooking Time: 3 minutes

1 cup steel-cut oats

2 cups water

1 cup nondairy milk

Pinch salt

½ tsp. vanilla extract

1 cinnamon stick

¼ cup raisins

¼ cup dried cherries

1 tsp. ground cinnamon

¼ cup toasted almonds

Honey, *optional*

1. Add all ingredients to the inner pot of the Instant Pot except the toasted almonds and honey.

2. Secure the lid and make sure the vent is turned to sealing. Cook for 3 minutes on High, using the manual function.

3. Let the pressure release naturally.

4. Remove cinnamon stick.

5. Add almonds, and honey if desired, and serve.

Calories: 276
Fat: 7g
Sodium: 53mg
Carbs: 46g
Sugar: 14g
Protein: 9g

Insta-Oatmeal

INSTANT POT

Hope Comerford, Clinton Township, MI

Makes 2 servings
Prep. Time: 2 minutes ⚖ Cooking Time: 3 minutes

1 cup gluten-free rolled oats
1 tsp. cinnamon
1½ Tbsp. maple syrup
Pinch salt
2 cups unsweetened almond milk

1. Place all ingredients in the inner pot of the Instant Pot and give a quick stir.

2. Secure the lid and set the vent to sealing.

3. Press the Manual button and set the cooking time to 3 minutes.

4. When the cooking time is up, manually release the pressure.

5. Remove the lid and stir. If the oatmeal is still too runny for you, let it sit a few minutes uncovered and it will thicken up.

Serving suggestion:

Top with ¼ cup of your favorite fruits, like banana slices, raspberries, chopped strawberries, or blueberries.

Calories: 270
Fat: 6.5g
Sodium: 307mg
Carbs: 44g
Sugar: 10g
Protein: 8.5g

Oatmeal Morning

Barbara Forrester Landis, Lititz, PA

Makes 6 servings
Prep. Time: 10 minutes   ♣   Cooking Time: 2½–6 hours   ♣   Ideal slow-cooker size: 3-qt.

I cup uncooked gluten-free
steel-cut oats

I cup dried cranberries

I cup walnuts

½ tsp. kosher salt

I Tbsp. cinnamon

2 cups water

2 cups fat-free nondairy milk
(almond, rice, etc.)

1. Combine all dry ingredients in slow cooker. Stir well.

2. Add water and milk and stir.

3. Cover. Cook on High 2½ hours, or on Low 5–6 hours.

Calories: 260
Fat: 12g
Sodium: 215mg
Carbs: 38g
Sugar: 14g
Protein: 6g

Grain and Fruit Cereal

Cynthia Haller, New Holland, PA

Makes 4–5 servings
Prep. Time: 5 minutes & Cooking Time: 3 hours & Ideal slow-cooker size: 4-qt.

⅓ cup uncooked quinoa

⅓ cup uncooked millet

⅓ cup uncooked brown rice

4 cups water

¼ tsp. salt

½ cup raisins or dried cranberries

¼ cup chopped nuts, *optional*

1 tsp. vanilla extract, *optional*

½ tsp. ground cinnamon, *optional*

1 Tbsp. maple syrup, *optional*

1. Wash the quinoa, millet, and brown rice and rinse well.

2. Place the grains, water, and salt in a slow cooker. Cook on Low until most of the water has been absorbed, about 3 hours.

3. Add dried fruit and any optional ingredients, then cook for 30 minutes more. If the mixture is too thick, add a little more water.

4. Serve hot or cold.

Serving suggestion:

Add a little nondairy milk to each bowl of cereal before serving.

Calories: 220
Fat: 2g
Sodium: 150mg
Carbs: 47g
Sugar: 11g
Protein: 5.5g

Soups, Stews, & Chilis

Chicken Tortilla Soup

SLOW COOKER

Becky Fixel, Grosse Pointe Farms, MI

Makes 10–12 servings

Prep. Time: 5 minutes   ⚜   Cooking Time: 7–8 hours   ⚜   Ideal slow-cooker size: 5-qt.

2-lb. boneless skinless chicken breast

32 oz. gluten-free chicken stock

14 oz. verde sauce

10-oz. can diced tomatoes with lime juice

15-oz. can sweet corn, drained

1 Tbsp. minced garlic

1 small onion, diced

1 Tbsp. chili pepper

½ tsp. fresh ground pepper

½ tsp. salt

½ tsp. oregano

1 Tbsp. dried jalapeño slices

1. Add all ingredients to your slow cooker.

2. Cook on Low for 7–8 hours.

3. Approximately 30 minutes before the end, remove your chicken and shred it into small pieces.

Serving suggestion:

Top with a dollop of nonfat plain Greek yogurt, shredded cheese, fresh jalapeños, or fresh cilantro.

Calories: 150
Fat: 3g
Sodium: 630mg
Carbs: 9g
Sugar: 4g
Protein: 20g

SLOW COOKER

Chicken Chickpea Tortilla Soup

Hope Comerford, Clinton Township, MI

Makes 4–6 servings
Prep. Time: 5 minutes ⚘ Cooking Time: 6 hours ⚘ Ideal slow-cooker size: 4-qt.

2 boneless skinless chicken breasts

2 (14½-oz.) cans petite diced tomatoes

15-oz. can garbanzo beans
(chickpeas), drained

6 cups gluten-free chicken stock

1 onion, chopped

4-oz. can diced green chilies

1 tsp. cilantro

3–4 fresh cloves garlic, minced

1 tsp. sea salt

1 tsp. pepper

1 tsp. cumin

1 tsp. paprika

1. Place all ingredients in slow cooker.

2. Cover and cook on Low for 6 hours.

3. Use two forks to pull apart chicken into shreds.

Serving suggestion:
Serve with a small dollop of nonfat Greek
yogurt, a little shredded cheddar, and
some baked blue corn tortilla chips.

Calories: 420
Fat: 9g
Sodium: 1400mg
Carbs: 48.5g
Sugar: 18.5g
Protein: 38.5g

Chicken and Vegetable Soup

SLOW COOKER

Hope Comerford, Clinton Township, MI

Makes 4–6 servings
Prep. Time: 15 minutes & Cooking Time: 7–8 hours & Ideal slow-cooker size: 5-qt.

1 lb. boneless skinless chicken, cut into bite-sized pieces

2 celery ribs, diced

1 small yellow squash, diced

4 oz. sliced mushrooms

2 large carrots, diced

1 medium onion, chopped

2 Tbsp. garlic powder

1 Tbsp. onion powder

1 Tbsp. basil

½ tsp. no-salt seasoning

1 tsp. salt

Black pepper to taste

32 oz. low-sodium chicken stock

1. Place the chicken, vegetables, and spices into the crock. Pour the chicken stock over the top.

2. Cover and cook on Low for 7–8 hours, or until vegetables are tender.

Calories: 160
Fat: 2g
Sodium: 700mg
Carbs: 13g
Sugar: 5g
Protein: 23g

Turkey Sausage and Cabbage Soup

Hope Comerford, Clinton Township, MI

Makes 8 servings
Prep. Time: 5 minutes ✿ Cooking Time: 17 minutes

2 Tbsp. olive oil

1½ cups chopped onions

2 cloves garlic, finely chopped

3 carrots, chopped in rounds

1 lb. bulk Italian turkey sausage, removed from casing

1 medium head green cabbage, shredded

2 (14½-oz.) cans no-salt-added diced tomatoes

1 Tbsp. dried basil

2 tsp. dried oregano

¼ tsp. black pepper

32 oz. low-sodium chicken stock or vegetable stock

1. Set the Instant Pot to Sauté and heat the olive oil in the inner pot.

2. Sauté the onions, garlic, and carrots for 2 minutes, then push them to the outer edges and add the sausage. Brown the sausage for about 3 minutes. Press Cancel.

3. Add the cabbage, tomatoes, basil, oregano, and black pepper. Finally, pour in the stock.

4. Secure the lid and set the vent to sealing.

5. Manually cook for 17 minutes on high pressure.

6. When the cooking time is over, manually release the pressure. Serve and enjoy!

Calories: 207
Fat: 11g
Sodium: 1173mg
Carbs: 14g
Sugar: 5g
Protein: 12g

Unstuffed Cabbage Soup

Colleen Heatwole, Burton, MI

Makes 4–6 servings
Prep. Time: 15 minutes   ℀   Cooking Time: 20 minutes

2 Tbsp. olive oil

1 lb. ground turkey or meatless crumbles

1 medium onion, diced

2 cloves garlic, minced

1 small head cabbage, chopped, cored, cut into roughly 2-inch pieces

6-oz. container tomato paste

32-oz. can diced tomatoes, with liquid

2 cups vegetable broth

1½ cups water

¾ cup brown rice

1–2 tsp. salt to taste

½ tsp. black pepper

1 tsp. oregano

1 tsp. parsley

1. Heat the olive oil in the inner pot of the Instant Pot using Sauté function. Add ground turkey or crumbles. Stir frequently for about 2 minutes.

2. Add onion and garlic and continue to sauté for 2 more minutes, stirring frequently.

3. Add chopped cabbage.

4. On top of cabbage, layer tomato paste, tomatoes with liquid, vegetable broth, water, rice, and spices.

5. Secure the lid and set vent to sealing. Using manual setting, select 20 minutes.

6. When time is up, let the pressure release naturally for 10 minutes, then do a quick release.

Variation:

You can use reduced-sodium broth and switch the added salt to a salt-free seasoning to reduce the sodium in this recipe.

Calories: 280
Fat: 6g
Sodium: 898mg
Carbs: 33g
Sugar: 6g
Protein: 23g

Veggie Minestrone

Dorothy VanDeest, Memphis, TN

Makes 8 servings
Prep. Time: 5 minutes ♣ Cooking Time: 4 minutes

2 Tbsp. olive oil

I large onion, chopped

I clove garlic, minced

4 cups low-sodium chicken or vegetable stock

16-oz. can kidney beans, rinsed and drained

14½-oz. can no-salt-added diced tomatoes

2 medium carrots, sliced thin

¼ tsp. dried oregano

¼ tsp. pepper

½ cup whole wheat elbow macaroni, uncooked

4 oz. fresh spinach

½ cup grated Parmesan cheese

1. Set the Instant Pot to the Sauté function and heat the olive oil.

2. When the olive oil is heated, add the onion and garlic to the inner pot and sauté for 5 minutes.

3. Press Cancel and add the stock, kidney beans, tomatoes, carrots, oregano, and pepper. Gently pour in the macaroni, but *do not stir*. Just push the noodles gently under the liquid.

4. Secure the lid and set the vent to sealing.

5. Manually set the cook time for 4 minutes on high pressure.

6. When the cooking time is over, manually release the pressure and remove the lid when the pin drops.

7. Stir in the spinach and let wilt a few minutes.

8. Sprinkle 1 Tbsp. grated Parmesan on each individual bowl of this soup. Enjoy!

Calories: 238
Fat: 6g
Sodium: 550mg
Carbs: 35g
Sugar: 6g
Protein: 12g

Slow-Cooker Tomato Soup

Becky Fixel, Grosse Pointe Farms, MI

Makes 8 servings
Prep. Time: 15 minutes & Cooking Time: 6 hours & Ideal slow-cooker size: 6-qt.

6–8 cups chopped fresh tomatoes

I medium onion, chopped

2 tsp. minced garlic

I tsp. basil

½ tsp. pepper

½ tsp. sea salt

½ tsp. red pepper flakes

2 Tbsp. Massel chicken bouillon

I cup water

¾ cup fat-free half-and-half

1. Combine the tomatoes, onion, spices, chicken bouillon, and water in slow cooker.

2. Cover and cook on Low for 6 hours.

3. Add in the fat-free half-and-half and combine all ingredients with an immersion blender. Serve hot.

Calories: 70
Fat: 0g
Sodium: 470mg
Carbs: 11g
Sugar: 6g
Protein: 1g

SLOW COOKER

Enchilada Soup

Melissa Paskvan, Novi, MI

Makes 6–8 servings
Prep. Time: 5 minutes ☙ Cooking Time: 6–8 hours ☙ Ideal slow-cooker size: 6-qt.

14½-oz. can diced tomatoes with green chilies or chipotles

12-oz. jar enchilada sauce

4 cups vegetable broth

1 small onion, chopped

3 cups sliced tri-colored peppers

10-oz. pkg. frozen corn

1 cup water

½ cup uncooked quinoa

1. Add all ingredients to slow cooker.

2. Cover and cook on Low for 6–8 hours.

Calories: 150
Fat: 2g
Sodium: 830mg
Carbs: 28g
Sugar: 7g
Protein: 4g

White Bean Soup

Esther H. Becker, Gordonville, PA

Makes 6 servings
Prep. Time: 5 minutes ⚓ *Cooking Time: 9 minutes*

2 (15½-oz.) cans white beans, rinsed and drained

4 cups water

3 cups low-fat, low-sodium chicken stock

1 tsp. grapeseed or olive oil

1 onion, diced

2 cups diced raw sweet potatoes (about 2 medium potatoes)

1 cup diced green bell pepper

¼ tsp. ground cloves

¼ tsp. black pepper

½ tsp. dried thyme

½ cup low-sugar ketchup

¼ cup molasses

1. Pour the beans, water, chicken stock, grapeseed oil, onion, sweet potato, bell pepper, ground cloves, black pepper, and thyme into the inner pot of the Instant Pot.

2. Secure the lid and set the vent to sealing.

3. Manually set the cook time to 9 minutes at high pressure.

4. When the cooking time is over, allow the pressure to release naturally. When the pin drops, remove the lid.

5. Stir in the ketchup and molasses. Add more water if you would like your soup to be thinner.

Calories: 325
Fat: 3g
Sodium: 886mg
Carbs: 62g
Sugar: 20g
Protein: 15g

Black Bean Soup with Fresh Salsa

Hope Comerford, Clinton Township, MI

Makes 6–8 servings
Prep. Time: 5 minutes   Cooking Time: 9 minutes

2 (15½-oz.) cans black beans, rinsed and drained

7 cups low-sodium chicken stock

5 cloves garlic, minced

1 Tbsp. chili powder

1½ tsp. cumin

1½ tsp. oregano

1 tsp. salt

1 tsp. olive oil

3 Tbsp. fat-free sour cream, *optional*

Salsa Ingredients:

⅓ cup fresh cilantro, washed and stemmed

½ onion, coarsely chopped

Juice of ½ lime

¼ tsp. salt

1. Place the beans, chicken stock, garlic, chili powder, cumin, oregano, salt, and olive oil into the inner pot of the Instant Pot.

2. Secure the lid and set the vent to sealing.

3. Manually set the cook time for 9 minutes on high pressure.

4. While the soup is cooking, puree the cilantro, onion, lime juice, and salt in a food processor until smooth. Place in a small bowl and keep refrigerated until serving time.

5. When the cooking time is over, let the pressure release naturally.

6. When the pin drops, remove the lid and scoop out about 1 cup of cooked beans with a slotted spoon and place in a bowl. Using an immersion blender, puree the beans then stir them back into the pot.

7. Spoon soup into serving bowls and serve with a bit of optional sour cream and fresh salsa on top.

Calories: 135
Fat: 2g
Sodium: 778mg
Carbs: 24g
Sugar: 1g
Protein: 9g

INSTANT POT

Mediterranean Lentil Soup

Marcia S. Myer, Manheim, PA

Makes 6 servings
Prep. Time: 10 minutes ♣ Cooking Time: 18 minutes

2 Tbsp. olive oil

2 large onions, chopped

I carrot, chopped

I cup uncooked lentils

½ tsp. dried thyme

½ tsp. dried marjoram

3 cups low-sodium chicken stock or vegetable stock

14½-oz. can diced no-salt-added tomatoes

¼ cup chopped fresh parsley

¼ cup sherry, *optional*

⅔ cup grated low-fat cheese, *optional*

1. Set the Instant Pot to the Sauté function, then heat up the olive oil.

2. Sauté the onions and carrot until the onions are translucent, about 5 minutes.

3. Press the Cancel button, then add the lentils, thyme, marjoram, chicken stock, and canned tomatoes.

4. Secure the lid and set the vent to sealing.

5. Manually set the cook time to 18 minutes at high pressure.

6. When the cooking time is over, manually release the pressure.

7. When the pin drops, stir in the parsley and sherry (if using).

8. When serving, add a sprinkle of grated low-fat cheese if you wish.

Calories: 282
Fat: 6g
Sodium: 303mg
Carbs: 18g
Sugar: 6g
Protein: 5g

Sweet Potato Soup with Kale

Hope Comerford, Clinton Township, MI

Makes 8 servings
Prep. Time: 5 minutes 🍃 *Cooking Time: 5 minutes*

I Tbsp. olive oil

I medium onion, chopped

2 cloves garlic, chopped

2 lb. sweet potatoes, diced

5 cups reduced-sodium chicken stock
or vegetable stock

14½-oz. can diced tomatoes

I bay leaf

I tsp. paprika

½ tsp. coriander

I sprig fresh rosemary

¼ tsp. pepper

5 oz. chopped kale

1. Set the Instant Pot to Sauté and heat up the olive oil in the inner pot.

2. Sauté the onion and garlic in the heated oil for 3 to 5 minutes.

3. Press Cancel and add the sweet potatoes, stock, diced tomatoes, bay leaf, paprika, coriander, rosemary, and pepper to the inner pot.

4. Secure the lid and set the vent to sealing.

5. Manually set the Instant Pot to cook for 5 minutes on high pressure.

6. When the cooking time is over, let the pressure release naturally for 10 minutes, then manually release the rest of the pressure.

7. When the pin drops, remove the lid and gently stir the kale into the soup. Let the soup sit for a few minutes so the kale can wilt, then serve.

Calories: 195
Fat: 4g
Sodium: 369mg
Carbs: 34g
Sugar: 8g
Protein: 7g

Chicken Chili Pepper Stew

Susan Kasting, Jenks, OK

Makes 4 servings
Prep. Time: 5 minutes ⚬ *Cooking Time: 8 minutes*

14½-oz. can low-sodium chicken stock
1 lb. boneless, skinless chicken breasts
4 cloves garlic, minced
1–2 jalapeño peppers, seeded and diced
1 medium red bell pepper, diced
1 medium carrot, sliced
15-oz. can no-salt-added corn, drained
1 tsp. cumin
2 Tbsp. chopped cilantro

1. Place all the ingredients, except the chopped cilantro, into the inner pot of the Instant Pot and secure the lid. Set the vent to sealing.

2. Manually set the cook time for 8 minutes on high pressure.

3. When the cooking time is over, let the pressure release naturally for 5 minutes, then manually release the pressure.

4. When the pin drops, remove the lid, remove the chicken, shred between 2 forks, then replace back in the inner pot. Stir.

5. Serve each bowl of stew with a sprinkling of chopped cilantro.

Calories: 258
Fat: 4g
Sodium: 156mg
Carbs: 26g
Sugar: 13g
Protein: 30g

Italian Shredded Pork Stew

Emily Fox, Bernville, PA

Makes: 6–8 servings
Prep. Time: 20 minutes ⚬ *Cooking Time: 8–10 hours* ⚬ *Ideal slow-cooker size: 5-qt.*

2 medium sweet potatoes, peeled and cubed

2 cups chopped fresh kale

1 large onion, chopped

3 cloves garlic, minced

2½–3½-lb. boneless pork shoulder butt roast

14-oz. can white kidney or cannellini beans, drained

1½ tsp. Italian seasoning

½ tsp. salt

½ tsp. pepper

3 (14½-oz.) cans chicken broth

Sour cream, *optional*

1. Place sweet potatoes, kale, onion, and garlic in slow cooker.

2. Place roast on vegetables.

3. Add beans and seasonings.

4. Pour the broth over the other ingredients.

5. Cover and cook on Low for 8 to 10 hours or until meat is tender.

6. Remove meat. Skim fat from cooking juices if desired. Shred pork with 2 forks and return to cooker. Heat through.

7. Garnish with sour cream if desired.

Calories: 383
Fat: 11g
Sodium: 1329mg
Carbs: 17g
Sugar: 6g
Protein: 42g

Moroccan Spiced Stew

SLOW COOKER

Melissa Paskvan, Novi, MI

Makes 6–8 servings
Prep. Time: 10 minutes ⚜ *Cooking Time: 8 hours* ⚜ *Ideal slow-cooker size: 5-qt.*

3 cups canned chopped tomatoes
3 cups gluten-free chicken stock
1 lb. lamb (ground or stew-cut pieces)
1 medium onion, chopped
⅛ tsp. fresh grated ginger
1½ tsp. cumin
¾ tsp. cinnamon
¾ tsp. turmeric
⅛–¼ tsp. cayenne pepper
½ cup shredded or chopped carrots
3 cups chopped sweet potato
Salt and pepper to taste

1. Place all ingredients in the crock and mix well to incorporate the spices.

2. Cover and cook on Low for 8 hours.

Serving suggestion:

Top with harissa for a zesty, warm flavor. Ladle this stew over brown rice or millet for a filling meal. Cook with ½ cup dried apricots or dates to impart a sweet taste.

Tip:

If you really want to seal in the warm spices, add 1 Tbsp. olive oil to a pan and brown just the outsides of the lamb pieces and cook with onions and spices. Then add in about 1 cup of the chicken stock to deglaze the pan and pour all ingredients from the pan to the slow cooker and add the remaining ingredients. This can also be made vegan using quinoa and chickpeas for the protein and substituting with vegetable stock. I add ½ cup rinsed quinoa to the recipe and 1 can garbanzo beans (chickpeas).

Calories: 330
Fat: 19g
Sodium: 415mg
Carbs: 225.5g
Sugar: 9.5g
Protein: 16g

Colorful Beef Stew

Hope Comerford, Clinton Township, MI

Makes 6 servings
Prep. Time: 20 minutes ⚹ Cooking Time: 8–9 hours ⚹ Ideal slow-cooker size: 4-qt.

2-lb. boneless beef chuck roast, trimmed of fat and cut into ¾-inch pieces

1 large red onion, chopped

2 cups gluten-free low-sodium beef broth

6-oz. can tomato paste

4 cloves garlic, minced

1 Tbsp. paprika

2 tsp. dried marjoram

½ tsp. black pepper

1 tsp. sea salt

1 red bell pepper, sliced

1 yellow bell pepper, sliced

1 orange bell pepper, sliced

1. Place all ingredients in the crock, except the sliced bell peppers, and stir.

2. Cover and cook on Low for 8–9 hours. Stir in sliced bell peppers during the last 45 minutes of cooking time.

Calories: 443
Fat: 15g
Sodium: 180mg
Carbs: 15g
Sugar: 7g
Protein: 50g

SLOW COOKER

Pumpkin Chili

Hope Comerford, Clinton Township, MI

Makes 8 servings
Prep. Time: 10 minutes ⚘ Cooking Time: 7–8 hours ⚘ Ideal slow-cooker size: 6-qt.

16-oz. can kidney beans, rinsed and drained

16-oz. can black beans, rinsed and drained

1 large onion, chopped

½ green pepper, chopped

1 lb. ground turkey, browned

15-oz. can pumpkin puree

4 cups fresh chopped tomatoes

3 Tbsp. garlic powder

1 Tbsp. ancho chili powder

1 tsp. salt

2 tsp. cumin

¼ tsp. pepper

4 Tbsp. gluten-free beef bouillon granules

5 cups water

1. Place the kidney beans, black beans, onion, and pepper in the crock.

2. Crumble the ground turkey over the top and spoon the pumpkin puree on top of that.

3. Add in the remaining ingredients and stir.

4. Cover and cook on Low for 7–8 hours.

Serving suggestion:
Garnish with roasted pumpkin seeds.

Calories: 300
Fat: 7g
Sodium: 650mg
Carbs: 39.5g
Sugar: 6g
Protein: 22.5g

White Chili

SLOW COOKER

Rebecca Plank Leichty, Harrisonburg, VA

Makes 6–8 servings
Prep. Time: 15 minutes   Cooking Time: 4–10 hours   Ideal slow-cooker size: 5-qt.

15-oz. can garbanzo beans (chickpeas), rinsed and drained

15-oz. can navy beans, drained, rinsed

15-oz. can pinto beans, drained, rinsed

2 (1-lb.) bags frozen corn

2 Tbsp. minced onions

1 red bell pepper, diced

3 tsp. minced garlic

3 tsp. ground cumin

½ tsp. salt

½ tsp. dried oregano

4 cups vegetable broth

1. Combine all ingredients in slow cooker.

2. Cover. Cook on Low for 8 to 10 hours or on High for 4 to 5 hours.

Tip:

For more zip, add 2 tsp. chili powder, or one or more chopped jalapeño peppers, to step 1.

Calories: 326
Fat: 3.5g
Sodium: 503mg
Carbs: 59g
Sugar: 13g
Protein: 19g

White and Green Chili

Hope Comerford, Clinton Township, MI

Makes 6 servings
Prep. Time: 20 minutes   ⚬   Cooking Time: 7–8 hours   ⚬   Ideal slow-cooker size: 4-qt.

1 lb. meatless crumbles

1 cup chopped onion

2 (15-oz.) cans great northern beans, rinsed and drained

1 (16-oz.) jar salsa verde (green salsa)

2 cups vegetable stock

4-oz. can green chilies

1½ tsp. ground cumin

1 tsp. sea salt

¼ tsp. black pepper

2 Tbsp. fresh chopped cilantro

⅓ cup plain nonfat Greek yogurt, *optional*

1. Place all ingredients in crock except cilantro and Greek yogurt. Stir.

2. Cover and cook on Low for 7–8 hours. Stir in cilantro and serve with a dollop of Greek yogurt, if desired.

Calories: 302
Fat: 2g
Sodium: 1580mg
Carbs: 48g
Sugar: 6g
Protein: 31g

Main Dishes

Chicken & Turkey

Garlic and Lemon Chicken

SLOW COOKER

Hope Comerford, Clinton Township, MI

Makes 5 servings

Prep. Time: 5 minutes ⚭ Cooking Time: 5–6 hours ⚭ Ideal slow-cooker size: 3- or 5-qt.

4–5 lb. boneless skinless chicken breasts or thighs

½ cup minced shallots

½ cup olive oil

¼ cup lemon juice

1 Tbsp. garlic paste (or use 1 medium clove garlic, minced)

1 Tbsp. no-salt seasoning

⅛ tsp. pepper

1. Place chicken in slow cooker.

2. In a small bowl, mix the remaining ingredients. Pour this mixture over the chicken in the crock.

3. Cover and cook on Low for 5–6 hours.

Calories: 450
Fat: 9g
Sodium: 260mg
Carbs: 3g
Sugar: 0g
Protein: 87g

INSTANT POT

Lemon and Olive Oil Chicken

Judy Gascho, Woodburn, OR

Makes 4 servings
Prep. Time: 15 minutes • Cooking Time: 7 minutes

2 Tbsp. olive oil

1 medium onion, chopped

4 cloves garlic, minced

½ tsp. paprika

1 Tbsp. chopped fresh parsley, or 1 tsp. dried parsley

½ tsp. pepper

2 lb. boneless chicken breasts or thighs

⅔ cup vegetable broth

⅓ cup lemon juice

1 tsp. salt

1–2 Tbsp. cornstarch

1 Tbsp. water

1. Set the Instant Pot to Sauté and add the olive oil.

2. Add the onion, garlic, paprika, parsley, and pepper to olive oil and sauté until onion starts to soften. Push onion to side of pot.

3. With the Instant Pot still at sauté, add the chicken and sear on each side for 3 to 5 minutes.

4. Mix broth, lemon juice, and salt together. Pour over chicken and stir to mix.

5. Put on lid and set Instant Pot, move vent to sealing and press Poultry. Set cook time for 7 minutes. Let depressurize naturally.

6. Remove chicken, leaving sauce in pot. Mix cornstarch in water and add to sauce. (Can start with 1 Tbsp. cornstarch, and use second one if sauce isn't thick enough.)

Serving suggestion:

Serve chicken and sauce over whole wheat noodles or brown rice.

Calories: 361
Fat: 13g
Sodium: 639mg
Carbs: 7g
Sugar: 2g
Protein: 52g

Lemony Chicken Thighs

Maria Shevlin, Sicklerville , NJ

Makes 3–5 servings
Prep. Time: 15 minutes   Cooking Time: 15 minutes

5 frozen bone-in chicken thighs
I cup vegetable broth
Juice of I lemon
I small onion, diced
5–6 cloves garlic, diced
2 Tbsp. olive oil
½ tsp. salt
¼ tsp. black pepper
I tsp. True Lemon® brand lemon pepper seasoning
I tsp. parsley flakes
¼ tsp. oregano
Zest of I lemon for garnish

1. Add all ingredients except lemon zest to the inner pot of the Instant Pot.

2. Lock the lid, make sure the vent is in sealing position, then press the Poultry button. Set to 15 minutes.

3. When cook time is up, let the pressure naturally release for 3 to 5 minutes, then manually release the rest.

4. For crispier chicken thighs, remove them from Instant Pot when cook time is up and place under the broiler for 2 to 3 minutes to brown.

5. Plate up and pour some of the sauce over the top with fresh lemon zest.

Calories: 336
Fat: 25g
Sodium: 354mg
Carbs: 3g
Sugar: 2g
Protein: 26g

Italian Crockpot Chicken

Andrea Maher, Dunedin, FL

Makes 6 servings
Prep. Time: 5 minutes ☙ Cooking Time: 3–8 hours ☙ Ideal slow-cooker size: 6-qt.

24-oz. boneless skinless chicken breast, cut into small pieces

3 cups garbanzo beans

16-oz. bag frozen spinach

2 cups mushrooms

2 Tbsp. Mrs. Dash™ Italian seasoning

1 cup low-sodium gluten-free chicken broth

1. Add all ingredients to the slow cooker.

2. Cover and cook on Low for 6–8 hours or High for 3–4 hours.

Calories: 280
Fat: 4g
Sodium: 270mg
Carbs: 25g
Sugar: 4g
Protein: 34g

Garlic Galore Rotisserie Chicken

Hope Comerford, Clinton Township, MI

Makes 4 servings
Prep. Time: 5 minutes & Cooking Time: 33 minutes

3-lb. whole chicken, innards removed

2 Tbsp. olive oil, *divided*

Salt to taste

Pepper to taste

20–30 cloves fresh garlic, peeled and left whole

1 cup vegetable broth

2 Tbsp. garlic powder

2 tsp. onion powder

½ tsp. basil

½ tsp. cumin

½ tsp. chili powder

1. Rub chicken with 1 Tbsp. of the olive oil and sprinkle with salt and pepper.

2. Place the garlic cloves inside the chicken. Use butcher's twine to secure the legs.

3. Press the Sauté button on the Instant Pot, then add the rest of the olive oil to the inner pot.

4. When the pot is hot, place the chicken inside. You are just trying to sear it, so leave it for about 4 minutes on each side.

5. Remove the chicken and set aside. Place the trivet at the bottom of the inner pot and pour in the vegetable broth.

6. Mix the remaining seasonings and rub the mixture all over the entire chicken.

7. Place the chicken back inside the inner pot, breast-side up, on top of the trivet and secure the lid to the sealing position.

8. Press the Manual button and use the +/- to set it for 25 minutes.

9. When the timer beeps, allow the pressure to release naturally for 15 minutes. If the lid will not open at this point, quick release the remaining pressure and remove the chicken.

10. Let the chicken rest for 5 to 10 minutes before serving.

Calories: 333
Fat: 23g
Sodium: 110mg
Carbs: 9g
Sugar: 1g
Protein: 24g

Thyme and Garlic Turkey Breast

SLOW COOKER

Hope Comerford, Clinton Township, MI

Makes 6–8 servings

Prep. Time: 10 minutes ⚜ *Cooking Time: 7–8 hours* ⚜ *Ideal slow-cooker size: 6- or 7-qt.*

4-lb. bone-in turkey breast, giblets removed if there are any, skin removed, washed and patted dry

¼ cup olive oil

1 Tbsp. balsamic vinegar

1 Tbsp. water

1 orange, juiced

6 cloves garlic, minced

1½ tsp. dried thyme

1 tsp. onion powder

1 tsp. kosher salt

1. Place turkey breast in crock.

2. Mix together the remaining ingredients and pour over the turkey breast. Rub it in on all sides with clean hands.

3. Cover and cook on Low for 7–8 hours.

Calories: 360
Fat: 11.5g
Sodium: 610mg
Carbs: 3.5g
Sugar: 1.5g
Protein: 58g

Artichoke-Tomato Chicken

SLOW COOKER

Barbara Jean Fabel, Wausau, WI

Makes 4 servings

Prep. Time: 10 minutes   Cooking Time: 4–6 hours   Ideal slow-cooker size: 3-qt.

1 yellow onion, thinly sliced

14-oz. jar marinated artichoke hearts, drained

14-oz. can low-sodium peeled tomatoes

6 Tbsp. red wine vinegar

1 tsp. minced garlic

½ tsp. salt

½ tsp. black pepper

4 boneless, skinless chicken breast halves

1. Combine all ingredients except chicken in slow cooker.

2. Place chicken in cooker, pushing down into vegetables and sauce until it's as covered as possible.

3. Cover. Cook on Low 4–6 hours.

4. Serve over rice.

Calories: 270
Fat: 8g
Sodium: 900mg
Carbs: 18g
Sugar: 4g
Protein: 30g

SLOW COOKER

Moist and Tender Turkey Breast

Marlene Weaver, Lititz, PA

Makes 12 servings
Prep. Time: 10 minutes & Cooking Time: 4–6 hours & Ideal slow-cooker size: 6- or 7-qt.

6–7-lb. bone-in turkey breast

4 fresh rosemary sprigs

4 cloves garlic, peeled

I Tbsp. brown sugar

½ tsp. coarsely ground pepper

¼ tsp. salt

1. Place turkey in a crock and place rosemary and garlic around it.

2. Combine the brown sugar, pepper, and salt; sprinkle over turkey.

3. Cover and cook on Low for 4–6 hours or until turkey is tender.

Calories: 300
Fat: 13.25g
Sodium: 160mg
Carbs: 1.5g
Sugar: 1g
Protein: 41.5g

Honey Balsamic Chicken

Hope Comerford, Clinton Township, MI

Makes 4–6 servings

Prep. Time: 5 minutes & Cooking Time: 7–8 hours & Ideal slow-cooker size: 5- or 6-qt.

4 cups chopped red potatoes

1½ tsp. kosher salt, *divided*

1 tsp. pepper, *divided*

8–10 boneless skinless chicken thighs

1 cup sliced red onion

1 pint cherry tomatoes

½ cup balsamic vinegar

¼ cup honey

2 Tbsp. olive oil

¼ tsp. red pepper flakes

½ tsp. dried thyme

½ tsp. dried rosemary

3 cloves garlic, minced

3 cups green beans

1. Spray crock with nonstick cooking spray.

2. Place potatoes in bottom of crock. Sprinkle with ½ tsp. of salt and ½ tsp. pepper.

3. Place chicken on top of potatoes and place sliced red onion and cherry tomatoes over the top.

4. Mix together the balsamic vinegar, honey, olive oil, 1 tsp. salt, remaining ½ tsp. pepper, red pepper flakes, thyme, rosemary, and garlic. Pour this mixture over the chicken, tomatoes, and potatoes.

5. Cook on Low for 7–8 hours, or until potatoes are tender.

6. About 20–30 minutes before serving, add the green beans on top.

Serving suggestion:
To serve, spoon the juices from the crock over the chicken and vegetables.

Calories: 285
Fat: 10g
Sodium: 540mg
Carbs: 33g
Sugar: 15g
Protein: 39g

Poached Chicken

SLOW COOKER

Mary E. Wheatley, Mashpee, MA

Makes 6 servings

Prep. Time: 15 minutes ⚹ Cooking Time: 7–8 hours ⚹ Ideal slow-cooker size: 4½-qt.

3-lb. whole chicken
I celery rib, cut into chunks
I carrot, sliced
I medium onion, sliced
I cup vegetable broth or water

1. Wash chicken. Pat dry with paper towels and place in slow cooker.

2. Place celery, carrot, and onion around chicken. Pour broth over all.

3. Cover and cook on Low for 7 to 8 hours, or until chicken is tender.

4. Remove chicken from pot and place on platter. When cool enough to handle, debone.

5. Strain broth into a container and chill.

6. Place chunks of meat in fridge or freezer until ready to use in salads or main dishes.

Calories: 748
Fat: 67g
Sodium: 213mg
Carbs: 3g
Sugar: 1g
Protein: 31g

Spanish Chicken

Natalia Showalter, Mt. Solon, VA

Makes 4–6 servings
Prep. Time: 15–20 minutes ❧ *Cooking Time: 5–6 hours* ❧ *Ideal slow-cooker size: 3- to 6-qt.*

8 chicken thighs, skinned

½–1 cup red wine vinegar, according to your taste preference

⅔ cups tamari, or low-sodium soy sauce

1 tsp. garlic powder

4 (6-inch) cinnamon sticks

1. Brown chicken slightly in nonstick skillet, if you wish, and then transfer to greased slow cooker.

2. Mix wine vinegar, tamari, and garlic powder together in a bowl. Pour over chicken.

3. Break cinnamon sticks into several pieces and distribute among chicken thighs.

4. Cover and cook on Low for 5 to 6 hours, or until chicken is tender but not dry.

Tip:

You can skip browning the chicken if you're in a hurry, but browning it gives the finished dish a better flavor.

Calories: 211
Fat: 12g
Sodium: 3071mg
Carbs: 3g
Sugar: 1g
Protein: 33g

Chicken Dinner in a Packet

INSTANT POT

Bonnie Whaling, Clearfield, PA

Makes 4 servings
Prep. Time: 10 minutes ⚭ Cooking Time: 15 minutes

1 cup water

4 (5-oz.) boneless, skinless chicken breast halves

2 cups sliced fresh mushrooms

2 medium carrots, cut in thin strips, about 1 cup

1 medium zucchini, unpeeled and sliced, about 1½ cups

2 Tbsp. olive oil or canola oil

2 Tbsp. lemon juice

1 Tbsp. fresh basil or 1 tsp. dried basil

¼ tsp. salt

¼ tsp. black pepper

1. Pour the water into the inner pot of the Instant Pot and place the trivet or a steamer basket on top.

2. Fold four 12 × 28-inch pieces of foil in half to make four 12 × 14-inch rectangles. Place one chicken breast half on each piece of foil.

3. Top with the mushrooms, carrots, and zucchini, dividing the vegetables equally between the chicken bundles.

4. In a small bowl, stir together the oil, lemon juice, basil, salt, and pepper.

5. Drizzle the oil mixture over the vegetables and chicken.

6. Pull up two opposite edges of foil. Seal with a double fold. Then fold in the remaining edges, leaving enough space for steam to build.

7. Place the bundles on top of the trivet, or inside the steamer basket.

8. Secure the lid and set the vent to sealing.

9. Manually set the cook time for 15 minutes at high pressure.

10. When the cooking time is over, let the pressure release naturally. When the pin drops, remove the lid.

11. Serve dinners in foil packets, or transfer to serving plate.

Calories: 275
Fat: 11g
Sodium: 218mg
Carbs: 35g
Sugar: 4g
Protein: 35g

Asian-Style Chicken with Pineapple

Andrea Maher, Dunedin, FL

Makes 6 servings
Prep. Time: 10 minutes ⚜ Cooking Time: 3–8 hours ⚜ Ideal slow-cooker size: 5- or 6-qt.

24-oz. boneless skinless chicken breast
cut into bite-size pieces

3 cups cubed pineapple

¼ cup Bragg® liquid aminos

1 Tbsp. brown sugar

½ cup chopped onion or 2 Tbsp.
onion powder

1 cup low-sodium gluten-free chicken
broth or stock

½ tsp. ground ginger

2 (16-oz.) bags frozen Szechuan mixed
veggies or any mixed veggies

1. Add all ingredients except for frozen veggies to the slow cooker.

2. Cover and cook on High 3–4 hours or Low 6–8 hours.

3. Add frozen veggies in the last 1–2 hours.

Calories: 280
Fat: 2g
Sodium: 830mg
Carbs: 38g
Sugar: 16g
Protein: 32g

Juicy Orange Chicken

Andrea Maher, Dunedin, FL

Makes 6 servings
Prep. Time: 10 minutes & Cooking Time: 3–8 hours & Ideal slow-cooker size: 5- or 6-qt.

18–24-oz. boneless, skinless chicken breast, cut into small pieces

1 cup orange juice, no additives

¼ cup honey

6 small oranges, peeled and sliced

¼ cup Bragg® liquid aminos

6 cups broccoli slaw

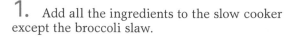

1. Add all the ingredients to the slow cooker except the broccoli slaw.

2. Cover and cook on High 3–4 hours or Low 6–8 hours.

3. Divide mixture between 6 mason jars.

4. Add 1 cup broccoli slaw to each mason jar.

5. Pour into a bowl when you're ready to eat!

Calories: 240
Fat: 2g
Sodium: 730mg
Carbs: 33g
Sugar: 25g
Protein: 26g

Easy Enchilada Shredded Chicken

Hope Comerford, Clinton Township, MI

Makes 10–14 servings
Prep. Time: 5 minutes   ⚜   Cooking Time: 5–6 hours   ⚜   Ideal slow-cooker size: 3- or 5-qt.

5–6 lb. boneless skinless chicken breast

14½-oz. can petite diced tomatoes

1 medium onion, chopped

8 oz. red enchilada sauce

½ tsp. salt

½ tsp. chili powder

½ tsp. basil

½ tsp. garlic powder

¼ tsp. pepper

1. Place chicken in the crock.

2. Add in the remaining ingredients.

3. Cover and cook on Low for 5–6 hours.

4. Remove chicken and shred it between two forks. Place the shredded chicken back in the crock and stir to mix in the juices.

Serving suggestion:

Serve over salad, brown rice, quinoa, sweet potatoes, nachos, or soft shell corn tacos. Add a dollop of yogurt and a sprinkle of fresh cilantro.

Calories: 240
Fat: 5g
Sodium: 340mg
Carbs: 4g
Sugar: 2g
Protein: 44g

Southwestern Shredded Chicken

Hope Comerford, Clinton Township, MI

SLOW COOKER

Makes 4 servings
Prep. Time: 8–10 minutes ⚶ *Cooking Time: 5–6 hours* ⚶ *Ideal slow-cooker size: 3-qt.*

1 ½ lb. boneless skinless chicken breast
1 Tbsp. chili powder
2 tsp. garlic powder
1 tsp. cumin
1 tsp. onion powder
½ tsp. kosher salt
¼ tsp. pepper
1 medium onion, chopped
14½-oz. can diced tomatoes
4-oz. can diced green chilies
½ cup nonfat Greek yogurt

Optional toppings:
Lettuce
Shredded cheese
Greek yogurt
Salsa

1. Place the chicken in the slow cooker.

2. Mix together the chili powder, garlic powder, cumin, onion powder, kosher salt, and pepper. Sprinkle this over both sides of the chicken.

3. Sprinkle the onion over the top of the chicken and pour the cans of diced tomatoes and green chilies over the top.

4. Cover and cook on Low for 5–6 hours.

5. Turn your slow cooker to warm. Remove the chicken and shred it between 2 forks.

6. Slowly whisk in the nonfat Greek yogurt with the juices in the crock. Replace the chicken in the crock and stir to mix in the juices.

Serving suggestion:
Serve this over brown rice or quinoa topped with some shredded lettuce, shredded cheese, and fresh salsa.

Calories: 250
Fat: 4g
Sodium: 600mg
Carbs: 13g
Sugar: 6g
Protein: 41g

Chicken Rice Bake

Nanci Keatley, Salem, OR

Makes 6 servings
Prep. Time: 8 minutes • Cooking Time: 22 minutes • Standing Time: 10 minutes

1 Tbsp. olive oil

1 cup finely diced onion

1 tsp. chopped garlic

1 cup chopped celery

2 lb. boneless, skinless chicken breasts,
cut into bite-sized pieces

1 cup chopped carrots

2 cups sliced fresh mushrooms

1½ cups uncooked brown rice

1½ tsp. salt

1 tsp. pepper

1 tsp. dill weed

1½ cups low-sodium chicken broth

1. Set the Instant Pot to the Sauté function and heat the oil in the inner pot.

2. Sauté the onion and garlic for 3 minutes. Add the celery and sauté an additional 3 minutes.

3. Press Cancel. Add the chicken and spread out evenly, Add the carrots and mushrooms and spread out evenly.

4. Pour the rice evenly on top and sprinkle with the seasonings. Last, pour in the chicken broth. Do not stir.

5. Manually set the cook time for 22 minutes on high pressure.

6. When the cooking time is over, manually release the pressure.

7. Allow to stand 10 minutes before serving.

Calories: 523
Fat: 12g
Sodium: 715mg
Carbs: 44g
Sugar: 4g
Protein: 57g

Chicken Curry with Rice

SLOW
COOKER

Jennifer Yoder Sommers, Harrisonburg, VA

Makes 6 servings

Prep. Time: 10 minutes   Cooking Time: 5–10 hours   Ideal slow-cooker size: 3- to 4-qt.

1½ lb. boneless, skinless chicken
thighs, quartered

1 onion, chopped

2 cups uncooked brown rice

2 Tbsp. curry powder

1¾ cups vegetable broth

1. Combine all ingredients in your slow cooker.

2. Cover and cook on Low for 8 to 10 hours, or on High for 5 hours, or until chicken is tender but not dry.

Variation:

Thirty minutes before the end of the cooking time, stir in 2 cups frozen peas.

Calories: 371
Fat: 11g
Sodium: 384mg
Carbs: 51g
Sugar: 1g
Protein: 26g

Spiced Lentils with Chicken and Rice

Janelle Reitz, Lancaster, PA

Makes 6 servings
Prep. Time: 10 minutes   ❧   Cooking Time: 15 minutes

1 Tbsp. olive oil

3-inch cinnamon stick

¾ tsp. ground cumin

6 cloves garlic, minced

1 onion, sliced

¾-lb. boneless, skinless chicken breast, cubed

1 cup uncooked brown rice, rinsed

½ cup brown lentils, rinsed

1 tsp. ground cardamom

2½ cups low-sodium, fat-free chicken broth

½ cup raisins

2 Tbsp. chopped fresh cilantro

½ cup toasted almonds, *optional*

1. Set the Instant Pot to the Sauté function and heat the oil.

2. Sauté the cinnamon stick, cumin, and garlic for 2 minutes.

3. Add the onion and sauté until tender, about 3 to 5 minutes.

3. Press Cancel. Add the chicken, brown rice, lentils, and cardamom, in that order. Pour in the chicken broth. Do not stir.

4. Secure the lid and set the vent to sealing.

5. Manually set the cook time for 15 minutes on high pressure.

6. When the cooking time is over, let the pressure release naturally for 15 minutes, then manually release the remaining pressure.

7. When the pin drops, remove the lid. Remove the cinnamon stick. Add the raisins, cilantro, and almonds (if using).

Calories: 329
Fat: 7g
Sodium: 193mg
Carbs: 41g
Sugar: 10g
Protein: 25g

SLOW COOKER

Turkey "Spaghetti" Quinoa

Hope Comerford, Clinton Township, MI

Makes 8–10 servings

Prep. Time: 10–15 minutes ⚜ *Cooking Time: 5 hours* ⚜ *Ideal slow-cooker size: 5- or 6-qt.*

2 lb. lean ground turkey

½ tsp. salt

⅛ tsp. pepper

1 tsp. garlic powder

1 tsp. onion powder

1 cup quinoa

1 cup chopped onion

1 cup shredded mozzarella cheese (for dairy-free, substitute with dairy-free cheese or leave out)

4 cups tomato sauce

2 cups water

1. Brown turkey with the salt, pepper, garlic powder, and onion powder.

2. Spray crock with nonstick spray.

3. Place ground turkey in bottom of crock. Top with quinoa, onion, and shredded mozzarella.

4. Pour tomato sauce and water into crock. Stir so everything is mixed.

5. Cover and cook on Low for 5 hours.

Calories: 300
Fat: 12.5g
Sodium: 800mg
Carbs: 20.5g
Sugar: 5g
Protein: 26g

Pork

Ginger Pork Chops

Mary Fisher, Leola, PA

Makes 4 servings
Prep. Time: 10 minutes   Cooking Time: 1 minute

⅓ cup low-sodium soy sauce or tamari

⅓ cup honey

2 cloves garlic, minced

Dash ground ginger

1 Tbsp. olive oil

4–5 thick-cut boneless pork chops
(1 inch to 1½ inches thick)

⅛ tsp. pepper

1 Tbsp. cornstarch

1 Tbsp. cold water

2 Tbsp. sliced green onions

Calories: 301
Fat: 10g
Sodium: 1390mg
Carbs: 27g
Sugar: 23g
Protein: 26g

1. In a bowl, mix the soy sauce, honey, garlic, and ginger. Set aside.

2. Set the Instant Pot to Sauté and heat the olive oil in the inner pot.

3. Season the pork chops on each side with a bit of pepper and then sear them in the inner pot. Only cook them for 1 to 2 minutes per side. Remove them and set them aside.

4. Add the sauce you made in the bowl earlier and stir, scraping the bottom of the pot with a wooden spoon.

5. Press Cancel. Place the pork chops into the sauce, including any juices the pork chops released while resting.

6. Secure the lid and set the vent to sealing. Set the Instant Pot to manually cook for 1 minute on high pressure.

7. When the cooking time is over, let the pressure release naturally for 5 minutes, then release the rest of the pressure manually.

8. When the pin drops, remove the lid and remove the pork chops. Set them aside on a clean plate or serving platter.

9. Mix the cornstarch and cold water. Set the Instant Pot to Sauté once more and whisk this mixture into the sauce in the inner pot. Let the sauce thicken to your liking, stirring often.

10. When you are ready to serve, pour some of the sauce over each pork chop and sprinkle with scallion.

SLOW COOKER

Raspberry Balsamic Pork Chops

Hope Comerford, Clinton Township, MI

Makes 4–6 servings
Prep. Time: 5 minutes ⚜ Cooking Time: 7–8 hours ⚜ Ideal slow-cooker size: 3-qt.

4–5 lb. thick-cut pork chops
¼ cup raspberry balsamic vinegar
2 Tbsp. olive oil
½ tsp. kosher salt
½ tsp. garlic powder
¼ tsp. basil
¼ cup water

1. Place pork chops in slow cooker.

2. In a small bowl, mix the remaining ingredients. Pour over the pork chops.

3. Cover and cook on Low for 7–8 hours.

Calories: 475
Fat: 16g
Sodium: 360mg
Carbs: 0g
Sugar: 0g
Protein: 76.5g

Brown Sugar Pork Chops

Andrea Maher, Dunedin, FL

Makes 6 servings

Prep. Time: 5 minutes   ♣   *Cooking Time: 3–8 hours*   ♣   *Ideal slow-cooker size: 5- or 6-qt.*

2 Tbsp. garlic powder

2 tsp. Dijon mustard

3 Tbsp. apple cider vinegar

¼ tsp. pepper

¼ tsp. kosher salt

⅓ cup water

¼ cup brown sugar or ¼ cup sugar-free maple syrup

3 cups pineapple slices

24 oz. boneless or bone-in pork chops

½ cup chopped celery

1. Combine all ingredients in slow cooker.

2. Cover and cook on High for 3–4 hours or on Low for 6–8 hours.

Calories: 230
Fat: 4g
Sodium: 180mg
Carbs: 21.5g
Sugar: 16g
Protein: 26.5g

Applesauce Pork Chops with Sweet Potatoes

Hope Comerford, Clinton Township, MI

Makes 4 servings
Prep. Time: 5 minutes & Cooking Time: 7 hours & Ideal slow-cooker size: 4-qt.

2 lb. thick-cut, bone-in pork chops

3 medium sweet potatoes, cut in 1-inch cubes

1½ cups natural no-sugar-added applesauce

¼ cup brown sugar, or sugar-free brown sugar substitute

1–2 Tbsp. minced onion

1 tsp. salt

¼ tsp. pepper

1. Place pork chops and sweet potatoes in crock.

2. In a bowl, mix the remaining ingredients. Pour this over the pork chops.

3. Cover and cook on Low for 7 hours.

Calories: 600
Fat: 30g
Sodium: 714mg
Carbs: 12g
Sugar: 16g
Protein: 50g

SLOW COOKER

Tropical Pork with Yams

Hope Comerford, Clinton Township, MI

Makes 6 servings
Prep. Time: 15 minutes ⚬ *Cooking Time: 7–8 hours* ⚬ *Ideal slow-cooker size: 5-qt.*

2–3-lb. pork loin

Salt to taste

Pepper to taste

20-oz. can crushed pineapple

¼ cup honey

¼ cup brown sugar

¼ cup apple cider vinegar

1 tsp. low-sodium soy sauce

4 yams, cut into bite-sized chunks

1. Spray the crock with nonstick spray.

2. Lay the pork loin at the bottom of the crock and sprinkle it with salt and pepper on both sides.

3. In a separate bowl, mix the pineapple, honey, brown sugar, apple cider vinegar, and soy sauce.

4. Place the chunks of yams over and around the pork loin and then pour the pineapple sauce over the top.

5. Cover and cook on Low for 7 to 8 hours.

Calories: 548
Fat: 23g
Sodium: 121mg
Carbs: 56g
Sugar: 30g
Protein: 31g

Pork and Sweet Potatoes

SLOW COOKER

Vera F. Schmucker, Goshen, IN

Makes 4 servings
Prep Time: 15 minutes ♣ Cooking Time: 4–4½ hours ♣ Ideal slow-cooker size: 4-qt.

4 pork loin chops

Salt to taste

Pepper to taste

4 sweet potatoes, cut in large chunks

2 onions, cut in quarters

½ cup apple cider

1. Place meat in bottom of slow cooker. Salt and pepper to taste.

2. Arrange sweet potatoes and onions over the pork.

3. Pour apple cider over all.

4. Cook on High for 30 minutes and then on Low for 3½ to 4 hours, or until meat and vegetables are tender but not dry.

Calories: 333
Fat: 8g
Sodium: 139mg
Carbs: 5g
Sugar: 15g
Protein: 15g

Korean-Inspired BBQ Shredded Pork

SLOW COOKER

Hope Comerford, Clinton Township, MI

Makes 8–10 servings
Prep. Time: 8–10 minutes ⚬ *Cooking Time: 8–10 hours* ⚬ *Ideal slow-cooker size: 3-qt.*

1 medium onion

1 McIntosh apple, peeled, cored

5 cloves garlic

¼ cup rice vinegar

1 tsp. gluten-free hot sauce

2 Tbsp. low-sodium gluten-free soy sauce

1 Tbsp. ginger

1 Tbsp. chili powder

¼ tsp. red pepper flakes

3 Tbsp. brown sugar

1 cup ketchup

2–3-lb. pork sirloin tip roast

1. In a food processor, puree the onion, apple, and garlic. Pour this mixture in a bowl and mix it with the rice vinegar, hot sauce, soy sauce, ginger, chili powder, red pepper flakes, brown sugar, and ketchup.

2. Place the pork roast into your crock. Pour the sauce over the top and turn it so it's covered on all sides.

3. Cover and cook on Low 8–10 hours.

4. Remove the pork roast and shred it between 2 forks. Return the shredded pork to the crock and mix it through the sauce.

Serving suggestion:

Serve over brown rice or quinoa with a side of bok choi sautéed in toasted sesame seed oil and red pepper flakes.

Calories: 210
Fat: 2.5g
Sodium: 560mg
Carbs: 15.5g
Sugar: 11g
Protein: 30g

Carnitas

Hope Comerford, Clinton Township, MI

Makes 12 servings
Prep. Time: 10 minutes ⚜ Cooking Time: 10–12 hours ⚜ Ideal slow-cooker size: 4-qt.

2-lb. pork shoulder roast

1½ tsp. kosher salt

½ tsp. pepper

2 tsp. cumin

5 cloves garlic, minced

1 tsp. oregano

3 bay leaves

2 cups gluten-free chicken stock

2 Tbsp. lime juice

1 tsp. lime zest

12 (6-inch) gluten-free white corn
tortillas

1. Place pork shoulder roast in crock.

2. Mix together the salt, pepper, cumin, garlic, and oregano. Rub it onto the pork roast.

3. Place the bay leaves around the pork roast, then pour in the chicken stock around the roast, being careful not to wash off the spices.

4. Cover and cook on Low for 10–12 hours.

5. Remove the roast with a slotted spoon, as well as the bay leaves. Shred the pork between 2 forks, then replace the shredded pork in the crock and stir.

6. Add the lime juice and lime zest to the crock and stir.

7. Serve on warmed white corn tortillas.

Calories: 220
Fat: 8g
Sodium: 390mg
Carbs: 14.5g
Sugar: 1g
Protein: 22.5g

Beef

Hungarian Beef with Paprika

SLOW COOKER

Maureen Csikasz, Wakefield, MA

Makes 9 servings

Prep. Time: 15 minutes & Cooking Time: 3–6 hours & Ideal slow-cooker size: oval 5- or 6-qt.

3-lb. boneless chuck roast

2–3 medium onions, coarsely chopped

5 Tbsp. sweet paprika

¾ tsp. salt

¼ tsp. black pepper

½ tsp. caraway seeds

1 clove garlic, chopped

½ green bell pepper, sliced

¼ cup water

½ cup nonfat plain Greek yogurt

Fresh parsley

1. Grease interior of slow-cooker crock.

2. Place roast in crock.

3. In a good-sized bowl, mix all ingredients together, except nonfat plain Greek yogurt and parsley.

4. Spoon evenly over roast.

5. Cover. Cook on High 3–4 hours, or on Low 5–6 hours, or until instant-read meat thermometer registers 140–145°F when stuck in center of meat.

6. When finished cooking, use sturdy tongs or 2 metal spatulas to lift meat to cutting board. Cover with foil to keep warm. Let stand 10–15 minutes.

7. Cut into chunks or slices.

8. Just before serving, dollop with nonfat plain Greek yogurt. Garnish with fresh parsley.

Calories: 250

Fat: 10.5g

Sodium: 320mg

Carbs: 6.5g

Sugar: 2.5g

Protein: 34.5g

Low-Fat Slow-Cooker Roast

Charlotte Shaffer, East Earl, PA

Makes 10 servings

Prep. Time: 15 minutes   ❧   Cooking Time: 3–8 hours   ❧   Ideal slow-cooker size: 6-qt.

3-lb. boneless beef roast

4 carrots, peeled and cut into
2-inch pieces

4 potatoes, cut into quarters

2 onions, quartered

1 cup gluten-free, low-sodium beef
broth or stock

1 tsp. garlic powder

1 tsp. Mrs. Dash® seasoning

½ tsp. salt

½ tsp. black pepper

1. Place roast in slow cooker.

2. Add carrots around edges, pushing them down so they reach the bottom of the crock.

3. Add potatoes and onions.

4. Mix together broth and seasonings and pour over roast.

5. Cover and cook on Low for 6–8 hours, or on High for 3–4 hours.

Calories: 340
Fat: 12g
Sodium: 275mg
Carbs: 20g
Sugar: 3g
Protein: 39g

Red Wine Apple Roast

Rose Hankins, Stevensville, MD

Makes 10 servings
Prep. Time: 15 minutes ❧ Cooking Time: 6–8 hours ❧ Ideal slow-cooker size: 4- or 5-qt.

3-lb. eye of round beef roast

3 cups thinly sliced onions

1½ cups chopped apples, peeled or unpeeled

3 cloves garlic, chopped

1 cup red wine

Salt and pepper to taste

1. Put roast in slow cooker. Layer onions, apples, and garlic on top of roast.

2. Carefully pour wine over roast without disturbing its toppings.

3. Sprinkle with salt and pepper to taste.

4. Cover. Cook on Low for 6 to 8 hours, or until meat is tender but not dry.

Calories: 364
Fat: 21g
Sodium: 85mg
Carbs: 13g
Sugar: 8g
Protein: 28g

Spicy Beef Roast

SLOW COOKER

Karen Ceneviva, Seymour, CT

Makes 10 servings
Prep. Time: 15–20 minutes   ♣   Cooking Time: 3–8 hours   ♣   Ideal slow-cooker size: 4- or 5-qt.

3-lb. eye of round roast, trimmed of fat

1–2 Tbsp. cracked black peppercorns

2 cloves garlic, minced

3 Tbsp. balsamic vinegar

¼ cup gluten-free reduced-sodium soy sauce or Bragg® liquid aminos

2 Tbsp. gluten-free Worcestershire sauce

2 tsp. dry mustard

1. Rub cracked pepper and garlic onto roast. Put roast in slow cooker.

2. Make several shallow slits in top of meat.

3. In a small bowl, combine remaining ingredients. Spoon over meat.

4. Cover and cook on Low for 6–8 hours, or on High for 3–4 hours, just until meat is tender, but not dry.

Calories: 240
Fat: 6g
Sodium: 530mg
Carbs: 2g
Sugar: 1g
Protein: 41.5g

Meat Sauce for Spaghetti

Becky Fixel, Grosse Pointe Farms, MI

Makes 6–8 servings
Prep. Time: 20 minutes ⚬ Cooking Time: 8 hours ⚬ Ideal slow-cooker size: 7-qt.

2 Tbsp. olive oil

28-oz. can crushed tomatoes

28-oz. can tomato sauce

15-oz. can Italian stewed tomatoes

6-oz. can tomato paste

2–3 Tbsp. basil

2 Tbsp. oregano

2 Tbsp. brown sugar

2 Tbsp. garlic paste (or 2 medium cloves, peeled and minced)

2 lb. extra-lean ground sirloin or lean ground turkey

1. Pour olive oil in the crock. Use a paper towel to rub it all around the inside.

2. Add all ingredients except ground sirloin or turkey. Stir together and put slow cooker on Low.

3. In a large skillet, brown your ground sirloin, and drain off any extra grease. Add this to your slow cooker.

4. Cook on Low for 8 hours.

Serving suggestion:

Serve over your favorite gluten-free pasta, zucchini "noodles," or cooked spaghetti squash "noodles."

Calories: 370
Fat: 17g
Sodium: 360mg
Carbs: 28.5g
Sugar: 19g
Protein: 29.5g

Beef with Broccoli

Genelle Taylor, Perrysburg, OH

Makes 4 servings
Prep. Time: 10 minutes   Cooking Time: 5–6 hours   Ideal slow-cooker size: 5- or 6-qt.

1 cup beef broth

½ cup low-sodium soy sauce

⅓ cup brown sugar, or sugar-free brown sugar substitute

1 Tbsp. sesame oil

3 cloves garlic, minced

1½-lb. boneless beef chuck roast or steak, sliced into thin strips

2 Tbsp. cornstarch

14-oz. bag frozen broccoli florets

1. In a mixing bowl, whisk together the beef broth, soy sauce, brown sugar, sesame oil, and garlic.

2. Lay the beef strips in slow cooker and pour the sauce over, tossing the strips to coat.

3. Cover and cook on Low for 5 to 6 hours

4. Remove 4 Tbsp. of the sauce and whisk it in a small bowl with cornstarch. Slowly stir this into slow cooker.

5. Add broccoli. Cook an additional 30 minutes.

Calories: 485
Fat: 23g
Sodium: 1600mg
Carbs: 27g
Sugar: 17g
Protein: 40g

Beef and Zucchini Casserole

Judi Manos, West Islip, NY

Makes 6 servings
Prep. Time: 12 minutes   ❧   Cooking Time: 22 minutes

2 tsp. canola oil

½ cup finely chopped onion

1 lb. 95%-lean ground beef

1 lb. (3 small) zucchini, cut into ¼-inch-thick slices

¼ lb. fresh mushrooms, sliced

14½-oz. can no-salt-added diced tomatoes

½ tsp. garlic powder

½ tsp. dried oregano

1 cup brown rice

2 cup water

¼ cup grated low-fat Parmesan cheese

1. Set the Instant Pot to Sauté and heat the oil in the inner pot.

2. Sauté the onion for about 3 minutes, then add the ground beef and sauté for about 8 more minutes, or until the beef is no longer pink.

3. Press Cancel. Add the remaining ingredients, except for the grated Parmesan cheese, into the inner pot in the order shown.

4. Secure the lid and set the vent to sealing.

5. Manually set the cook time for 22 minutes on high pressure.

6. When the cooking time is over, let the pressure release naturally.

7. When the pin drops, remove the lid and stir in the Parmesan cheese. Serve and enjoy!

Calories: 287
Fat: 7g
Sodium: 226mg
Carbs: 37g
Sugar: 4g
Protein: 22g

Steak and Rice Dinner

Susan Scheel, West Fargo, ND

Makes 8 servings
Prep. Time: 15–20 minutes ❧ *Cooking Time: 4–6 hours* ❧ *Ideal slow-cooker size: 5-qt.*

I cup uncooked wild rice, rinsed and drained

I cup chopped celery

I cup chopped carrots

2 (4-oz.) cans mushrooms, drained

I large onion, chopped

½ cup slivered almonds

3 beef bouillon cubes

2½ tsp. seasoned salt

2-lb. boneless round steak, cut in bite-sized pieces

3 cups water

1. Layer ingredients in slow cooker in order listed. Do not stir.

2. Cover. Cook on Low for 4 to 6 hours.

3. Stir before serving.

Tip:

To reduce the sodium in this recipe, swap the seasoned salt for your favorite salt-free seasoning blend.

Calories: 290
Fat: 11g
Sodium: 1042mg
Carbs: 21g
Sugar: 3g
Protein: 29g

Slow-Cooker Swiss Steak

Joyce Bowman, Lady Lake, FL

Makes 4 servings

Prep. Time: 10 minutes ⚜ *Cooking Time: 7 hours* ⚜ *Ideal slow-cooker size: 3-qt.*

1-lb. round steak, ¾–1-inch thick, cubed

16-oz. can low-sodium stewed tomatoes

3 carrots, halved lengthwise

2 potatoes, quartered

1 medium onion, quartered

Garlic powder to taste, *optional*

1. Add all ingredients to slow cooker in the order they are listed.

2. Cover and cook on Low for 7 hours, or until meat and vegetables are tender, but not overcooked or dry.

Calories: 237
Fat: 7g
Sodium: 364mg
Carbs: 18g
Sugar: 7g
Protein: 26g

Meatless

Mushroom Risotto

Hope Comerford, Clinton Township, MI

Makes 4 servings
Prep. Time: 7 minutes   Cooking Time: 6 minutes

1 Tbsp. extra-virgin olive oil

½ cup finely chopped onion

2 cloves garlic, minced

½ cup chopped baby bella mushrooms

½ cup chopped shiitake mushrooms

¼ tsp. salt

⅛ tsp. pepper

1 cup uncooked arborio rice

2 cups low-sodium chicken or vegetable stock

½ cup frozen peas, thawed

¼ cup freshly grated low-fat Parmesan cheese

1 Tbsp. butter or margarine, *optional*

Tip:

The nutrition information for this recipe is calculated using chicken stock, but to keep this dish vegetarian, use vegetable stock instead.

1. Set the Instant Pot to the Sauté function and heat the oil in the inner pot.

2. Sauté the onion and garlic for 3 minutes. Add the mushrooms, salt, and pepper, and continue sautéing for an additional 3 to 4 minutes.

3. Press Cancel. Stir in the rice and chicken stock. Secure the lid and set the vent to sealing.

4. Manually set the cook time for 6 minutes on high pressure.

5. When the cooking time is over, manually release the pressure.

6. When the pin drops, remove the lid and stir in the peas, grated Parmesan, and butter or margarine (if using). Let the peas heat through for about 2 minutes, then serve.

Calories: 186
Fat: 6g
Sodium: 385mg
Carbs: 26g
Sugar: 4g
Protein: 8g

Quinoa with Spinach

Karen Ceneviva, New Haven, CT

Makes 4 servings
Prep. Time: 2 minutes 🍃 Cooking Time: 1 minute

1½ cups raw quinoa

2¼ cups water

3 Tbsp. freshly squeezed lemon juice

2 Tbsp. extra-virgin olive oil

¼ tsp. sea salt

Pepper to taste, *optional*

2 cups fresh spinach leaves, well washed, dried, and chopped

3 large green onions, thinly sliced

3 Tbsp. fresh dill

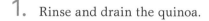

1. Rinse and drain the quinoa.

2. Pour the quinoa and water into the inner pot of the Instant Pot. Secure the lid and set the vent to sealing.

3. Manually set the time for 1 minute on high pressure.

4. When the cooking time is over, let the pressure release naturally.

5. When the pin drops, remove the lid. Stir in the lemon juice, olive oil, sea salt, and pepper (if using).

6. Stir in the spinach, green onions, and dill.

7. Serve warm, or at room temperature.

Calories: 339
Fat: 11g
Sodium: 118mg
Carbs: 52g
Sugar: 9g
Protein: 10g

Spinach Stuffed Tomatoes

Charlotte Hagner, Montague, MI

Makes 4 main-dish servings
Prep. Time: 15 minutes & Cooking Time: 1 minute

4 large, firm tomatoes

1 Tbsp. olive oil

10-oz. package frozen spinach, thawed and squeezed dry

2 Tbsp. finely chopped onion

½ cup fat-free half-and-half

2 egg whites, or egg substitute equivalent to 1 egg

1½ cups water

Tip:

You may replace the olive oil with canola or grapeseed oil if you wish.

Calories: 110
Fat: 5g
Sodium: 117mg
Carbs: 11g
Sugar: 6g
Protein: 6g

1. Slice off the top of each tomato. Remove the pulp and seeds.

2. Set the Instant Pot to the Sauté function and heat the olive oil in the inner pot.

3. Sauté the spinach and onion in the inner pot for about 5 minutes.

4. Hit Cancel on the Instant Pot.

5. In a small bowl, combine the half-and-half and egg whites or egg substitute.

6. Stir in the sautéed spinach and onion. Spoon this mixture into the tomatoes.

7. Add the water to the inner pot and place the trivet on top.

8. Arrange the filled tomatoes on top of the trivet inside the inner pot.

9. Secure the lid and set the vent to sealing.

10. Manually set the cook time for 1 minute on high pressure.

11. When the cooking time is over, manually release the pressure.

12. When the pin drops, remove the lid and very carefully remove the trivet from the inner pot with oven mitts.

13. Carefully place the stuffed tomatoes on a serving platter. Serve warm and enjoy!

Spinach Pie

Mary Ellen Musser, Reinholds, PA

Makes 4 main-dish servings

Prep. Time: 5 minutes ⚜ Cooking Time: 25 minutes ⚜ Standing Time: 10 minutes

2 cups low-sodium fat-free cottage cheese

10-oz. package frozen chopped spinach, thawed and squeezed dry

1 cup reduced-fat mozzarella cheese, shredded

Egg substitute equivalent to 4 eggs, or 8 egg whites, beaten

⅓ cup (1½ ounces) grated low-fat Parmesan cheese

1 tsp. dried oregano

1 cup water

1. Mix all the ingredients in a large bowl.

2. Spoon into a lightly greased 7-inch round pan. Cover it tightly with foil.

3. Pour the water into the inner pot of the Instant Pot. Place the trivet on top.

4. Place the filled pan on top of the trivet.

5. Secure the lid and set the vent to sealing.

6. Manually set the cook time to 25 minutes on high pressure.

7. When the cooking time is over, let the pressure release naturally for 10 minutes, then manually release the remaining pressure.

8. When the pin drops, remove the lid and carefully lift the trivet and pan out with oven mitts. Remove the foil. Allow to stand for 10 minutes before cutting.

Calories: 304
Fat: 12g
Sodium: 1036mg
Carbs: 14g
Sugar: 6g
Protein: 35g

Spicy Orange Tofu

Sue Hamilton, Benson, AZ

Makes 3 servings

Prep. Time: 5 minutes   ⚓   Cooking Time: 5 hours   ⚓   Ideal slow-cooker size: 3-qt.

12½ oz. extra-firm gluten-free tofu, drained and diced

1½ cups orange marmalade (natural or low-sugar is best)

1 tsp. powdered ginger

1 tsp. minced garlic

1 Tbsp. balsamic vinegar

1 tsp. sriracha hot chili sauce or to taste

12-oz. bag of mixed stir-fry vegetables

1. Place the drained tofu in the crock.

2. Mix together the marmalade, ginger, garlic, vinegar, and hot chili sauce. Pour over the tofu, but don't mix as it will break up the tofu.

3. Cover and cook on Low for 4 hours.

4. Add the stir-fry vegetables on top and cook for one hour longer.

Serving suggestion:
Serve over brown rice.

Calories: 590
Fat: 7.5g
Sodium: 150mg
Carbs: 125.5g
Sugar: 97.5g
Protein: 16g

Double Corn Tortilla Bake

Kathy Keener Shantz, Lancaster, PA

Makes 4 servings
Prep. Time: 15 minutes & Cooking Time: 2–3 hours & Ideal slow-cooker size: 3- or 4-qt.

8 corn tortillas, *divided*

1½ cups shredded Monterey Jack cheese, *divided*

1 cup corn, fresh, frozen, or canned (drained of water), *divided*

4 green onions, sliced, about ½ cup, *divided*

2 eggs, beaten

1 cup buttermilk

4-oz. can diced green chilies

1. Grease interior of slow-cooker crock.

2. Tear 4 tortillas into bite-sized pieces. Scatter evenly over bottom of crock.

3. Top with half the cheese, half the corn, and half the green onions.

4. Repeat layers.

5. In a mixing bowl, stir together eggs, buttermilk, and chilies. Gently pour over tortilla mixture.

6. Cover. Cook on Low for 2 to 3 hours, or until knife inserted in center comes out clean.

Calories: 406
Fat: 20g
Sodium: 472mg
Carbs: 40g
Sugar: 8g
Protein: 20g

Mexi Rotini

Jane Geigley, Lancaster, PA

Makes 6 servings
Prep. Time: 30 minutes   Cooking Time: 4½ hours   Ideal slow-cooker size: 4-qt.

1 cup water

3 cups partially cooked whole wheat rotini

12-oz. package frozen mixed vegetables

10-oz. can Ro*Tel® diced tomatoes with green chilies

4-oz. can green chilies, undrained

1 lb. meatless crumbles

½ cup low-fat shredded cheddar cheese

1. Combine all ingredients in slow cooker except shredded cheddar.

2. Cover and cook on Low for 4 hours.

3. Top with the low-fat shredded cheddar, then let cook covered for an additional 20 minutes or so.

Calories: 239
Fat: 2g
Sodium: 852mg
Carbs: 38g
Sugar: 4g
Protein: 26g

SLOW
COOKER

Baked Ziti

Hope Comerford, Clinton Township, MI

Makes 8 servings
Prep. Time: 15 minutes ⚘ Cooking Time: 4 hours ⚘ Ideal slow-cooker size: 5-qt.

28-oz. can low-sodium
crushed tomatoes

15-oz. can low-sodium tomato sauce

1½ tsp. Italian seasoning

1 tsp. garlic powder

1 tsp. onion powder

1 tsp. pepper

1 tsp. sea salt

1 lb. whole wheat ziti or rigatoni pasta,
uncooked, *divided*

1 cup low-fat shredded mozzarella
cheese, *divided*

1. Spray crock with nonstick spray.

2. In a bowl, mix crushed tomatoes, tomato sauce, Italian seasoning, garlic powder, onion powder, pepper, and salt.

3. In the bottom of the crock, pour ⅓ of the pasta sauce.

4. Add ½ of the pasta on top of the sauce.

5. Add another ⅓ of your pasta sauce.

6. Spread ½ of the mozzarella cheese on top of that.

7. Add the remaining pasta, the remaining sauce, and the remaining cheese on top of that.

8. Cover and cook on Low for 4 hours.

Calories: 398
Fat: 11g
Sodium: 1054mg
Carbs: 54g
Sugar: 7g
Protein: 23g

Faked-You-Out Alfredo

SLOW COOKER

Sue Hamilton, Benson, AZ

Makes 4 servings
Prep. Time: 5 minutes ❧ *Cooking Time: 6 hours* ❧ *Ideal slow-cooker size: 3-qt.*

1 lb. bag of frozen cauliflower

13½-oz. can light coconut milk

½ cup diced onion

2 cloves garlic, minced

1 Tbsp. vegetable stock concentrate

Salt and pepper to taste

1. Place the frozen cauliflower, coconut milk, onion, garlic, and the vegetable stock concentrate in your crock. Stir mixture to blend in the stock concentrate.

2. Cover and cook on Low for 6 hours.

3. Place cooked mixture in blender and process until smooth.

4. Add salt and pepper to taste.

Serving suggestion:

Serve over cooked whole-wheat or gluten free pasta, or any zucchini or spaghetti squash "noodles."

Calories: 205
Fat: 5g
Sodium: 300mg
Carbs: 36g
Sugar: 7g
Protein: 7g

Lentils with Cheese

Kay Nussbaum, Salem, OR
Laura R. Showalter, Dayton, VA
Natalia Showalter, Mt. Solon, VA

Makes 6 servings
Prep. Time: 2 minutes ⚶ Cooking Time: 10 minutes

1½ cups raw lentils, rinsed

3 cups water

½ tsp. salt

¼ tsp. pepper

⅛ tsp. dried marjoram

⅛ tsp. dried sage

⅛ tsp. dried thyme

2 large onions, chopped

2 cloves garlic, minced

14½-oz. can low-sodium diced tomatoes

2 large carrots, sliced ⅛-inch thick

½ cup thinly sliced celery

1 bell pepper, chopped, *optional*

1 cup (4 oz.) low-fat, low-sodium shredded cheddar cheese

1. Place the lentils, water, salt, pepper, marjoram, sage, thyme, onions, garlic, tomatoes, carrots, celery, and bell pepper, if using, into the inner pot of the Instant Pot.

2. Secure the lid and set the vent to sealing.

3. Manually set the cook time for 10 minutes on high pressure.

4. When the cooking time is over, manually release the pressure.

5. When the pin drops, remove the lid. Stir in the shredded cheddar cheese.

Calories: 98
Fat: 2g
Sodium: 496mg
Carbs: 13g
Sugar: 4g
Protein: 8g

Seafood

Simple Salmon

INSTANT POT

Evie Hershey, Atglen, PA

Makes 4 servings

Prep. Time: 3 minutes ⚹ Cooking Time: 3–5 minutes

1 cup water

1 tsp. olive oil

1-lb. salmon fillet, fresh or frozen

½ tsp. Old Bay® Seasoning

½ tsp. fine bread crumbs

1. Pour the water into the inner pot of the Instant Pot. Place the trivet on top.

2. In a 7-inch round baking pan, spread the olive oil on the bottom.

3. Season the salmon fillet with the Old Bay Seasoning and place it skin-side down in the baking pan. Sprinkle the bread crumbs on top.

4. Place the baking pan on top of the trivet in the inner pot.

5. Secure the lid and set the vent to sealing.

6. Manually set the cook time on high pressure for 3 minutes if fresh or 5 minutes if frozen.

7. When the cooking time is over, manually release the pressure.

8. When the pin drops, remove the lid and carefully remove the trivet from the inner pot with oven mitts. Check to make sure the fillet is at 145°F.

Calories: 229

Fat: 17g

Sodium: 245mg

Carbs: 10g

Sugar: 1g

Protein: 25g

INSTANT POT

Maple-Glazed Salmon

Jenelle Miller, Marion, SD

Makes 6 servings
Prep. Time: 5 minutes   ✿   Cooking Time: 3 minutes

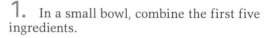

2 tsp. paprika

2 tsp. chili powder

½ tsp. ground cumin

½ tsp. brown sugar

½ tsp. kosher salt

6 (4-oz.) salmon fillets

1 Tbsp. maple syrup

1 cup water

1. In a small bowl, combine the first five ingredients.

2. Rub the fillets with the seasoning mixture.

3. Spray a 7-inch round baking pan with nonstick cooking spray, and place the salmon in the pan skin-side down. Drizzle the fish with the maple syrup.

4. Pour the water into the inner pot of the Instant Pot and place the trivet on top. Place the baking pan on top of the trivet.

5. Secure the lid and set the vent to sealing.

6. Manually set the cook time for 3 minutes on high pressure.

7. When the cooking time is over, manually release the pressure.

8. When the pin drops, remove the lid and carefully remove the trivet from the inner pot with oven mitts. Check to make sure the fillets are at 145°F.

Calories: 250
Fat: 15g
Sodium: 253mg
Carbs: 3g
Sugar: 2g
Protein: 23g

Honey Lemon Garlic Salmon

INSTANT POT

Judy Gascho, Woodburn, OR

Makes 4 servings
Prep. Time: 15 minutes   Cooking Time: 8 minutes

5 Tbsp. olive oil

3 Tbsp. honey

2–3 Tbsp. lemon juice

3 cloves garlic, minced

4 (3–4-oz.) fresh salmon fillets

Salt and pepper to taste

1–2 Tbsp. minced parsley (dried or fresh)

Lemon slices, *optional*

1½ cups water

1. Mix olive oil, honey, lemon juice, and minced garlic in a bowl.

2. Place each salmon fillet on a piece of foil big enough to wrap up the piece of fish.

3. Brush each fillet generously with the olive oil mixture.

4. Sprinkle with salt, pepper, and parsley flakes.

5. Top each with a thin slice of lemon if desired.

6. Wrap each fillet and seal well at top.

7. Add water to the inner pot of your Instant Pot and place the trivet in the pot.

8. Place wrapped fillets on the trivet.

9. Close the lid and turn valve to sealing.

10. Cook on manual at high pressure for 5 to 8 minutes for smaller pieces, or for 10 to 12 minutes if they are large.

11. Carefully release pressure manually at the end of the cooking time.

12. Unwrap and enjoy.

Calories: 352
Fat: 22g
Sodium: 81mg
Carbs: 15g
Sugar: 13g
Protein: 26g

Lemon Pepper Tilapia

Karen Ceneviva, New Haven, CT

Makes 4 servings
Prep. Time: 1 minute & Cooking Time: 2–4 minutes

1 cup water

4 (6-oz.) tilapia fillets, fresh or frozen

2 tsp. lemon pepper seasoning

1. Pour the water into the inner pot of the Instant Pot.

2. Sprinkle the fillets with lemon pepper seasoning on both sides.

3. Place the steamer basket into the inner pot and carefully arrange the tilapia in the basket.

4. Secure the lid and set the vent to sealing.

5. Manually set the cook time for 2 minutes on high pressure for fresh fish, or 4 minutes for frozen fish.

6. When the cooking time is over, manually release the pressure.

7. When the pin drops, remove the lid. Make sure the fish is at 145°F.

Calories: 163
Fat: 3g
Sodium: 248mg
Carbs: 0g
Sugar: 0g
Protein: 34g

INSTANT
POT

Herbed Fish Fillets

Patricia Howard, Green Valley, AZ

Makes 4 servings
Prep. Time: 5 minutes 🌿 Cooking Time: 5–9 minutes

1 cup water

4 fish fillets (hake, cod, or mahi-mahi), fresh or frozen

Juice of ½ lemon

1 tsp. dill weed

1 tsp. dried basil

1 tsp. no-salt seasoning

1½ tsp. parsley flakes

4 thin slices lemon

1. Pour the water into the inner pot of the Instant Pot and place the trivet on top.

2. Arrange the fillets in a 7-inch round baking pan. It's all right if they overlap a bit.

3. In a small bowl, mix the lemon juice, dill, basil, no-salt seasoning, and parsley. Pour this over the fillets and place a slice of lemon on top of each fillet.

4. Secure the lid and set the vent to sealing.

5. Manually set the cook time for 5 minutes on high pressure for fresh fish, or 9 minutes for frozen fish.

6. When the cooking time is over, manually release the pressure.

7. When the pin drops, remove the lid. Make sure the fish is at 145°F.

Calories: 99
Fat: 1g
Sodium: 62mg
Carbs: 1.5g
Sugar: 0.5g
Protein: 20g

Spiced Cod

Hope Comerford, Clinton Township, MI

Makes 4–6 servings
Prep. Time: 8 minutes ⚘ *Cooking Time: 2 hours* ⚘ *Ideal slow-cooker size: 4- or 5-qt.*

4–6 cod filets
½ cup thinly sliced red onion
1½ tsp. garlic powder
1½ tsp. onion powder
½ tsp. cumin
¼ tsp. ancho chili pepper
1 lime, juiced
⅓ cup vegetable broth

1. Place fish in the crock. Place the onion on top.

2. Mix together the remaining ingredients and pour over the fish.

3. Cover and cook on Low for 2 hours, or until fish flakes easily with a fork.

Serving suggestion:
Serve on a bed of quinoa or brown rice.

Calories: 200
Fat: 1.5g
Sodium: 190mg
Carbs: 3.5g
Sugar: 1g
Protein: 41.5g

Cajun Catfish

SLOW COOKER

Hope Comerford, Clinton Township, MI

Makes 4 servings
Prep. Time: 5 minutes   Cooking Time: 2 hours   Ideal slow-cooker size: 6-qt.

4–6 oz. catfish fillet

2 tsp. paprika

1 tsp. black pepper

1 tsp. oregano

1 tsp. dried thyme

½ tsp. garlic powder

½ tsp. kosher salt

½ tsp. parsley flakes

¼ tsp. cayenne pepper

1 Tbsp. coconut oil

1. Pat the catfish filets dry.

2. Mix together the paprika, black pepper, oregano, thyme, garlic powder, salt, parsley flakes, and cayenne.

3. Place parchment paper in your crock and push it down so it forms against the inside of the crock. Place the coconut oil in the crock.

4. Coat each side of the catfish fillet with the spice mixture, then place them in the crock.

5. Cover and cook on Low for about 2 hours, or until the fish flakes easily with a fork.

Calories: 240
Fat: 13.5g
Sodium: 460mg
Carbs: 1.5g
Sugar: 0g
Protein: 26.5g

Hot Tuna Macaroni Casserole

Dorothy VanDeest, Memphis, TN

Makes 6 servings
Prep. Time: 15 minutes & Cooking Time: 2–6 hours & Ideal slow-cooker size: 3-qt.

2 (6-oz.) cans tuna, water-packed,
rinsed and drained

1½ cups cooked macaroni

½ cup finely chopped onions

¼ cup finely chopped green
bell peppers

4-oz. can sliced mushrooms, drained

10-oz. pkg. frozen cauliflower,
partially thawed

½ cup low-sodium, fat-free
chicken broth

1. Combine all ingredients in slow cooker. Stir well.

2. Cover. Cook on Low for 4 to 6 hours or on High for 2 to 3 hours.

Calories: 193
Fat: 5g
Sodium: 339mg
Carbs: 16g
Sugar: 2g
Protein: 20g

Side Dishes

Quinoa with Almonds and Cranberries

Colleen Heatwole, Burton, MI

Makes 4 servings
Prep. Time: 5 minutes 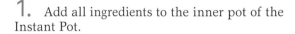 *Cooking Time: 2 minutes*

I cup quinoa, rinsed well
½ cup roasted slivered almonds
I vegetable bouillon cube
1½ cups water
¼ tsp. salt, *optional*
I cinnamon stick
½ cup dried cranberries or cherries
I bay leaf

1. Add all ingredients to the inner pot of the Instant Pot.

2. Secure the lid and make sure vent is on sealing. Cook 2 minutes using high pressure in Manual mode.

3. Turn off pot and let the pressure release naturally for 10 minutes. After 10 minutes are up, release pressure manually.

4. Remove cinnamon stick and bay leaf.

5. Fluff with fork and serve.

Calories: 282
Fat: 9g
Sodium: 365mg
Carbs: 43g
Sugar: 12g
Protein: 9g

SLOW COOKER

Quinoa with Vegetables

Hope Comerford, Clinton Township, MI

Makes 4–6 servings
Prep. Time: 10 minutes ⚭ Cooking Time: 4–6 hours ⚭ Ideal slow-cooker size: 3-qt.

2 cups quinoa

4 cups vegetable stock

½ cup chopped onion

1 Tbsp. olive oil

1 medium red pepper, chopped

1 medium yellow pepper, chopped

1 medium carrot, chopped

3 cloves garlic, minced

½ tsp. sea salt

¼ tsp. pepper

1 Tbsp. chopped fresh cilantro

1. Place quinoa, vegetable stock, onion, olive oil, red pepper, yellow pepper, carrot, garlic, salt, and pepper into crock and stir.

2. Cook on Low for 4–6 hours or until liquid is absorbed and quinoa is tender.

3. Top with fresh cilantro to serve.

Calories: 315
Fat: 7g
Sodium: 690mg
Carbs: 53g
Sugar: 4g
Protein: 10.5g

Artichokes and Brown Rice

INSTANT POT

Betty K. Drescher, Quakertown, PA

Makes 6 servings
Prep. Time: 5 minutes ☙ Cooking Time: 15 minutes

1 Tbsp. extra-virgin olive oil

14½-oz. can artichokes, drained and cut into chunks

1 cup raw brown rice

1 cup low-sodium vegetable stock

1. Set the Instant Pot to Sauté and heat the oil in the inner pot.

2. Sauté the artichokes in the olive oil for about 5 minutes. Press Cancel.

3. Add the rice and vegetable stock to the inner pot. Secure the lid and set the vent to sealing.

4. Manually set the cook time for 15 minutes on high pressure.

5. When the cooking time is over, let the pressure release naturally for 5 minutes, then manually release the remaining pressure.

6. When the pin drops, remove the lid and fluff the rice with a fork. Serve and enjoy!

Calories: 165
Fat: 3g
Sodium: 156mg
Carbs: 31g
Sugar: 1g
Protein: 5g

Cilantro Lime Rice

Cindy Herren, West Des Moines, IA

Makes 6–8 servings
Prep. Time: 5 minutes   Cooking Time: 3 minutes

2 cups extra-long-grain rice or
jasmine rice

4 cups water

2 Tbsp. olive oil or butter, *divided*

2 tsp. salt

¼ cup fresh chopped cilantro

1 lime, juiced

1. Add the rice, the water, 1 Tbsp. oil, and the salt to the inner pot of the Instant Pot and stir.

2. Secure the lid and set the vent to sealing.

3. Manually set the cook time to 3 minutes on high pressure.

4. When the cooking time is over, let the pressure release naturally for 10 minutes, then manually release the remaining pressure.

5. When the pin drops, remove the lid. Fluff the rice with a fork. Add the chopped cilantro, lime juice, and remaining oil and mix well.

Calories: 201
Fat: 4g
Sodium: 486mg
Carbs: 38g
Sugar: 0g
Protein: 3g

INSTANT POT

Hometown Spanish Rice

Beverly Flatt-Getz, Warriors Mark, PA

Makes 6–8 servings
Prep. Time: 8 minutes 🔥 Cooking Time: 3 minutes

I Tbsp. olive oil

I large onion, chopped

I bell pepper, chopped

2 cups long-grain rice, rinsed

1½ cups low-sodium chicken stock

28-oz. can low-sodium stewed tomatoes

Grated Parmesan cheese, *optional*

1. Set the Instant Pot to Sauté and heat the oil in the inner pot.

2. Sauté the onion and bell pepper in the inner pot for about 3 to 5 minutes.

3. Add the rice and continue to sauté for about 1 more minute. Press Cancel.

4. Add the chicken stock and tomatoes with their juices into the inner pot, in that order.

5. Secure the lid and set the vent to sealing.

6. Manually set the cook time for 3 minutes on high pressure.

7. When the cooking time is over, let the pressure release naturally for 10 minutes, then manually release the remaining pressure.

8. When the pin drops, remove the lid. Fluff the rice with a fork.

9. Sprinkle with Parmesan cheese, if using, just before serving.

Calories: 284
Fat: 5g
Sodium: 518mg
Carbs: 53g
Sugar: 4g
Protein: 7g

Savory Rice

SLOW COOKER

Jane Geigley, Lancaster, PA

Makes 6–8 servings
Prep. Time: 10 minutes ❧ *Cooking Time: 3–4 hours* ❧ *Ideal slow-cooker size: 4-qt.*

2 cups uncooked short-grain brown rice

5 cups water

I Tbsp. coconut oil

½ tsp. ground thyme

2 Tbsp. dried parsley

2 tsp. garlic powder

I tsp. dried basil

I tsp. salt

1. Mix rice, water, coconut oil, thyme, parsley, garlic powder, basil, and salt.

2. Pour into slow cooker. Cover.

3. Cook on High for 3–4 hours or until water is absorbed.

Calories: 230
Fat: 2.5g
Sodium: 340mg
Carbs: 46g
Sugar: 0g
Protein: 4g

Instant Spaghetti Squash

Hope Comerford, Clinton Township, MI

Makes 4–6 servings
Prep. Time: 5 minutes ⚖ Cooking Time: 10 minutes

1 medium spaghetti squash
1 cup water

1. Cut the spaghetti squash in the middle (not lengthwise) so that it will fit in the inner pot.

2. Pour the water into the inner pot of the Instant Pot and place the trivet on top.

3. Place the squash pieces, cut-side down, on the trivet.

4. Secure the lid and set the vent to sealing.

5. Manually set the cook time for 10 minutes on high pressure.

6. When the cooking time is over, manually release the pressure.

7. When the pin drops, remove the lid.

8. Carefully remove the squash, and, using a fork, shred the squash inside the skin. To do this, move your fork clockwise around the inside of the squash.

Serving suggestions:
Serve with a little bit of butter or margarine and a touch of salt and pepper. Spaghetti squash is a delicious and healthy alternative to traditional spaghetti noodles.

Calories: 16
Fat: 0g
Sodium: 9mg
Carbs: 3g
Sugar: 1g
Protein: 0g

INSTANT POT

Perfect Sweet Potatoes

Brittney Horst, Lititz, PA

Makes 4–6 servings
Prep. Time: 5 minutes ⚬ Cooking Time: 15 minutes

4–6 medium sweet potatoes

1 cup water

1. Scrub the skin of the sweet potatoes with a brush until clean. Pour the water into the inner pot of the Instant Pot. Place the steamer basket in the bottom of the inner pot. Place the sweet potatoes on top of the steamer basket.

2. Secure the lid and turn the valve to seal.

3. Select the Manual mode and set to pressure cook on high for 15 minutes.

4. Allow pressure to release naturally (about 10 minutes).

5. Once the pressure valve lowers, remove the lid and serve immediately.

Tips:

You may also use a trivet if you do not have a steamer basket.

You can store cooked sweet potatoes in the refrigerator for 3 to 4 days in an airtight container.

Super-large sweet potatoes need more than 15 minutes! I tried one mega sweet potato, and it was not cooked in the center. Maybe 20 minutes will do.

Calories: 130
Fat: 0g
Sodium: 72mg
Carbs: 26g
Sugar: 5g
Protein: 2g

Thyme Roasted Sweet Potatoes

SLOW COOKER

Hope Comerford, Clinton Township, MI

Makes 6 servings

Prep. Time: 20 minutes   Cooking Time: 2–3 hours   Ideal slow-cooker size: 4-qt.

4–6 medium sweet potatoes, peeled, cubed

3 Tbsp. olive oil

5–6 large cloves garlic, minced

⅓ cup fresh thyme leaves

½ tsp. kosher salt

¼ tsp. red pepper flakes

1. Place all ingredients into the crock and stir.

2. Cover and cook on High for 2–3 hours, or until potatoes are tender.

Calories: 160
Fat: 7g
Sodium: 250mg
Carbs: 23.5g
Sugar: 4.5g
Protein: 2g

Quick and Light Sweet Potato Wedges

MarJanita Geigley, Lancaster, PA

Makes 4 servings
Prep. Time: 15 minutes ☙ Cooking Time: 3–5 hours ☙ Ideal slow-cooker size: 3-qt.

4 sweet potatoes, cut into wedges

2 Tbsp. olive oil

2 tsp. Italian seasoning

3 Tbsp. light gluten-free Italian dressing

1 Tbsp. minced garlic

1. Combine all ingredients in sealable plastic bag and shake well.

2. Pour into slow cooker and cook on Low for 3–5 hours.

Serving suggestion:

To make a dipping sauce, mix Greek yogurt, sriracha sauce, and minced garlic to taste.

Calories: 180

Fat: 7g

Sodium: 190mg

Carbs: 28.5g

Sugar: 6.5g

Protein: 2.5g

Sweet Potato Puree

Colleen Heatwole, Burton, MI

Makes 4–6 servings
Prep. Time: 10 minutes   *Cooking Time: 6 minutes*

3 lb. sweet potatoes, peeled and cut into roughly 2-inch cubes

1 cup water

2 Tbsp. olive oil

1 tsp. salt

2 tsp. honey

2 tsp. lemon juice

½ tsp. cinnamon

⅛ tsp. nutmeg, *optional*

1. Place sweet potatoes and water in the inner pot of the Instant Pot.

2. Secure the lid, make sure vent is at sealing, then cook for 6 minutes on High, using the manual setting.

3. Manually release the pressure when cook time is up.

4. Drain sweet potatoes and place in large mixing bowl. Mash with potato masher or hand mixer.

5. Once thoroughly mashed, add remaining ingredients.

6. Taste and adjust seasonings to taste.

7. Serve immediately while still hot.

Calories: 244
Fat: 5g
Sodium: 446mg
Carbs: 48g
Sugar: 12g
Protein: 4g

White Beans with Sun-Dried Tomatoes

SLOW COOKER

Steven Lantz, Denver, CO

Makes 4–6 servings

Prep. Time: 15 minutes ⚘ Cooking Time: 4½–6½ hours ⚘ Ideal slow-cooker size: 4-qt.

2 cups uncooked great northern beans, rinsed

2 cloves garlic, minced or pressed

1 onion, chopped

6 cups water

½ tsp. salt

⅛ tsp. pepper

1 cup chopped sun-dried tomatoes in oil, drained

2-oz. can sliced black olives, drained

¼ cup low-fat grated Parmesan cheese

1. Mix all ingredients except tomatoes, olives, and cheese in 4- or 5-qt. slow cooker.

2. Cover and cook on High for 4 to 6 hours or until beans are tender.

3. Mash some of the beans to thicken mixture. Stir in tomatoes and olives. Cook for 20 to 30 minutes more, until thoroughly heated.

4. Ladle into bowls and sprinkle each with Parmesan cheese.

Calories: 114
Fat: 3g
Sodium: 322mg
Carbs: 25 g
Sugar: 4g
Protein: 8g

Aunt Twila's Beans

SLOW COOKER

Mary Louise Martin, Boyd, WI

Makes 10–12 servings
Prep. Time: 15 minutes   Cooking Time: 10 hours   Ideal slow-cooker size: 5-qt.

5 cups dry pinto beans
2 tsp. ground cumin
1 medium yellow onion, minced
4 cloves garlic, minced
9 cups water
3 tsp. salt
3 Tbsp. lemon juice

1. Combine beans, cumin, onion, garlic, and water in slow cooker.

2. Cook on Low for 8 hours.

3. Add salt and lemon juice. Stir. Cook on Low for another 2 hours.

Calories: 310
Fat: 1g
Sodium: 650mg
Carbs: 56.5g
Sugar: 2.5g
Protein: 19g

Potatoes with Parsley

Colleen Heatwole, Burton, MI

Makes 4 servings
Prep. Time: 10 minutes   Cooking Time: 5 minutes

3 Tbsp. olive oil, *divided*

2 lb. medium red potatoes (about 2 oz. each), halved lengthwise

1 clove garlic, minced

½ tsp. salt

½ cup vegetable broth

2 Tbsp. chopped fresh parsley

1. Place 1 Tbsp. olive oil in the inner pot of the Instant Pot and select Sauté.

2. When olive oil is hot, add potatoes, garlic, and salt, stirring well.

3. Sauté for 4 minutes, stirring frequently.

4. Add vegetable broth and stir well.

5. Seal lid, make sure vent is on sealing, then select manual for 5 minutes on High.

6. When cooking time is up, manually release the pressure.

7. Strain potatoes then toss with remaining olive oil and chopped parsley. Serve immediately.

Calories: 251
Fat: 11g
Sodium: 289mg
Carbs: 36g
Sugar: 3g
Protein: 4.5g

Slow-Cooker Beets

Hope Comerford, Clinton Township, MI

Makes 4–6 servings

Prep. Time: 10 minutes ❧ *Cooking Time: 3–4 hours* ❧ *Ideal slow-cooker size: 3-qt.*

4–6 large beets, scrubbed well and tops removed

3 Tbsp. olive oil, *divided*

1 tsp. sea salt, *divided*

¼ tsp. pepper, *divided*

3 Tbsp. balsamic vinegar, *divided*

1 Tbsp. lemon juice, *divided*

1. Use foil to make a packet around each beet.

2. Divide the olive oil, salt, pepper, balsamic vinegar, and lemon juice evenly between each packet. Seal each packet by folding the top together.

3. Place each beet packet into the slow cooker.

4. Cover and cook on Low for 3–4 hours, or until the beets are tender when poked with a knife.

5. Remove each beet packet from the crock and allow to cool and let the steam escape. Once cool enough to handle, use a paring knife to gently peel the skin off each beet. Cut into bite-sized pieces and serve with juice from the packet over the top.

Calories: 140
Fat: 8.5g
Sodium: 570mg
Carbs: 14.5g
Sugar: 10.5g
Protein: 2g

Corn on the Cob

SLOW
COOKER

Donna Conto, Saylorsburg, PA

Makes 3–4 servings
Prep. Time: 10 minutes ⚘ Cooking Time: 2–3 hours ⚘ Ideal slow-cooker size: 5- or 6-qt.

6–8 ears of corn (in husk)

½ cup water

1. Remove silk from corn, as much as possible, but leave husks on.

2. Cut off ends of corn so ears can stand in the cooker.

3. Add water.

4. Cover. Cook on Low 2–3 hours.

Serving suggestion:

Serve with butter, salt and pepper, and fresh herbs, if desired.

Calories: 154
Fat: 2g
Sodium: 30mg
Carbs: 34g
Sugar: 6g
Protein: 6g

INSTANT POT

Rosemary Carrots

Orpha Herr, Andover, NY

Makes 6 servings
Prep. Time: 10 minutes ⚘ Cooking Time: 2 minutes

1 cup water
1½ lb. carrots, sliced
1 Tbsp. olive oil
½ cup diced green bell pepper
1 tsp. dried rosemary, crushed
¼ tsp. coarsely ground black pepper

1. Pour the water into the inner pot of the Instant Pot, place the sliced carrots into a steamer basket, and put the steamer basket into the inner pot.

2. Secure the lid and set the vent to sealing.

3. Manually set the cook time for 2 minutes on high pressure.

4. When the cooking time is over, manually release the pressure. Wait for the pin to drop and remove the lid. Press Cancel.

5. Carefully remove the carrots, set aside, and empty the water out of the inner pot. Wipe dry.

6. Place the inner pot back into the Instant Pot, then press Sauté and heat the oil in the inner pot.

7. Add the green bell pepper and sauté for 5 minutes, then add the carrots and stir.

8. Sprinkle the carrots and green pepper with rosemary and black pepper. Serve and enjoy!

Calories: 70
Fat: 2.5g
Sodium: 79mg
Carbs: 12g
Sugar: 6g
Protein: 1g

Brussels Sprouts with Pimentos

Donna Langton, Rapid City, SD

Makes 8 servings

Prep. Time: 10 minutes ⚜ *Cooking Time: 6 hours* ⚜ *Ideal slow-cooker size: 3½- or 4-qt.*

2 lb. Brussels sprouts

¼ tsp. dried oregano

½ tsp. dried basil

2-oz. jar pimentos, drained

¼ cup, or 1 small can sliced black olives, drained

1 Tbsp. olive oil

½ cup water

1. Combine all ingredients in slow cooker.

2. Cook on Low 6 hours, or until sprouts are just tender.

Calories: 70
Fat: 2.5g
Sodium: 60mg
Carbs: 11g
Sugar: 2.5g
Protein: 4g

Broccoli and Bell Peppers

Frieda Weisz, Aberdeen, SD

Makes 8 servings

Prep. Time: 20 minutes ⚘ *Cooking Time: 4–5 hours* ⚘ *Ideal slow-cooker size: 3½- or 4-qt.*

2 lb. fresh broccoli, trimmed and chopped into bite-sized pieces

1 clove garlic, minced

1 green or red bell pepper, cut into thin slices

1 onion, peeled and cut into slices

4 Tbsp. low-sodium gluten-free soy sauce or Bragg® liquid aminos

½ tsp. salt

Dash of black pepper

1 Tbsp. sesame seeds, as garnish, *optional*

1. Combine all ingredients except sesame seeds in slow cooker.

2. Cook on Low for 4–5 hours. Top with sesame seeds.

Serving suggestion:
Serve over cooked brown rice.

Calories: 60
Fat: 0.5g
Sodium: 690mg
Carbs: 10.5g
Sugar: 3.5g
Protein: 4.5g

Greek-Style Green Beans

Diann J. Dunham, State College, PA

Makes 6 servings
Prep. Time: 5 minutes ⚜ *Cooking Time: 2–5 hours* ⚜ *Ideal slow-cooker size: 4-qt.*

20 oz. whole or cut-up frozen green
beans (not French cut)

2 cups low-sodium tomato sauce

2 tsp. dried onion flakes, *optional*

Pinch dried marjoram or oregano

Pinch ground nutmeg

Pinch cinnamon

1. Combine all ingredients in slow cooker, mixing thoroughly.

2. Cover and cook on Low for 2 to 4 hours if the beans are defrosted, or for 3 to 5 hours on Low if the beans are frozen, or until the beans are done to your liking.

Calories: 47
Fat: 0.5g
Sodium: 386mg
Carbs: 11g
Sugar: 5g
Protein: 2g

Lemony Garlic Asparagus

SLOW COOKER

Hope Comerford, Clinton Township, MI

Makes 4 servings

Prep. Time: 5 minutes   ♣   Cooking Time: 1½–2 hours   ♣   Ideal slow-cooker size: 2- or 3-qt.

I lb. asparagus, bottom inch (tough part) removed

I Tbsp. olive oil

1½ Tbsp. lemon juice

3–4 cloves garlic, peeled and minced

¼ tsp. salt

⅛ tsp. pepper

1. Spray crock with nonstick spray.

2. Lay asparagus at bottom of crock and coat with the olive oil.

3. Pour the lemon juice over the top, then sprinkle with the garlic, salt, and pepper.

4. Cover and cook on Low for 1½–2 hours.

Serving suggestion:

Garnish with diced pimento, garlic, and lemon zest.

Calories: 60
Fat: 3.5g
Sodium: 150mg
Carbs: 5.5g
Sugar: 2.5g
Protein: 2.5g

Desserts

Fudgy Secret Brownies

SLOW COOKER

Juanita Weaver, Johnsonville, IL

Makes 8 servings
Prep. Time: 10 minutes   ♣   Cooking Time: 1½–2 hours   ♣   Ideal slow-cooker size: 6- or 7-qt.

4 oz. unsweetened chocolate

¾ cup coconut oil

¾ cup frozen diced okra, partially thawed

3 large eggs

1½ cups xylitol or your choice of sweetener

1 tsp. pure vanilla extract

¼ tsp. mineral salt

¾ cup coconut flour

½–¾ cup coarsely chopped walnuts or pecans, *optional*

1. Melt chocolate and coconut oil in small saucepan.

2. Put okra and eggs in blender. Blend until smooth.

3. Measure all other ingredients in mixing bowl.

4. Pour melted chocolate and okra over the dry ingredients and stir with fork just until mixed.

5. Pour into greased slow cooker.

6. Cover and cook on High for 1½–2 hours.

Calories: 450
Fat: 31.5g
Sodium: 130mg
Carbs: 35.5g
Sugar: 2g
Protein: 6.5g

Black Bean Brownies

Juanita Weaver, Johnsonville, IL

Makes 6–8 servings
Prep. Time: 5 minutes ⚜ *Cooking Time: 1–1½ hours* ⚜ *Ideal slow-cooker size: 5- or 6-qt.*

15-oz. can of black beans, rinsed
and drained

6 eggs

⅓ cup cocoa powder

1½ tsp. aluminum-free baking powder

½ tsp. baking soda

2 Tbsp. coconut oil

2 tsp. pure vanilla extract

⅓ cup Greek yogurt or cottage cheese

¾ cup xylitol or your choice
of sweetener

¼ tsp. salt

1. Put all ingredients in a food processor or blender. Blend until smooth.

2. Pour into greased slow cooker.

3. Cover and cook for 1–1½ hours on High.

4. Cool in crock. For best taste, chill before serving.

Calories: 230
Fat: 8.5g
Sodium: 360mg
Carbs: 29g
Sugar: .5g
Protein: 11g

Zucchini Chocolate Chip Bars

SLOW COOKER

Hope Comerford, Clinton Township, MI

Makes 8–10 servings
Prep Time: 10 minutes ❧ Cooking Time: 2–3 hours
Cooling Time: 30 minutes ❧ Ideal slow-cooker size: 3-qt.

3 eggs
¾ cup turbinado sugar
1 cup all-natural applesauce
3 tsp. vanilla extract
3 cups whole wheat flour
1 tsp. baking soda
½ tsp. baking powder
2 tsp. cinnamon
¼ tsp. salt
2 cups peeled and grated zucchini
1 cup dark chocolate chips

1. Spray the crock with nonstick spray.

2. Mix together the eggs, sugar, applesauce, and vanilla.

3. In a separate bowl, mix together the flour, baking soda, baking powder, cinnamon, and salt. Add this to the wet mixture and stir just until everything is mixed well.

4. Stir in the zucchini and chocolate chips

5. Pour this mixture into the crock.

6. Cover and cook on Low for 2–3 hours. Let it cool in crock for about 30 minutes, then flip it over onto a serving platter or plate. It should come right out.

Calories: 400
Fat: 12.5g
Sodium: 240mg
Carbs: 71.5g
Sugar: 34.5g
Protein: 7.5g

Bananas Foster

SLOW COOKER

Hope Comerford, Clinton Township, MI

Makes 6 servings

Prep. Time: 5–10 minutes ☙ *Cooking Time: 1½–2 hours* ☙ *Ideal slow-cooker size: 4-qt.*

1 Tbsp. olive oil

3 Tbsp. raw honey

3 Tbsp. fresh lemon juice

¼ tsp. cinnamon

Dash nutmeg

5 bananas (not green, but just yellow), sliced into ½-inch-thick slices

1. Combine the first five ingredients in the slow cooker.

2. Add the bananas and stir to coat them evenly.

3. Cover and cook on Low for 1½–2 hours.

Calories: 141
Fat: 3g
Sodium: 2mg
Carbs: 32g
Sugar: 21g
Protein: 1g

SLOW
COOKER

Dates in Cardamom Coffee Syrup

Margaret W. High, Lancaster, PA

Makes 12 servings
Prep. Time: 15 minutes ⚬ *Cooking Time: 7–8 hours* ⚬ *Ideal slow-cooker size: 3-qt.*

2 cups pitted, whole dried dates

2½ cups very strong, hot coffee

2 Tbsp. turbinado sugar

15 whole green cardamom pods

4-inch cinnamon stick

Plain Greek yogurt, for serving

1. Combine dates, coffee, sugar, cardamom, and cinnamon stick in slow cooker.

2. Cover and cook on High for 1 hour. Remove lid and continue to cook on High for 6–7 hours until sauce has reduced.

3. Strain the cardamom pods and cinnamon sticks from the sauce, then pour dates and sauce into container and chill in fridge.

4. To serve, put a scoop of Greek yogurt in a small dish and add a few dates on top. Drizzle with a little sauce.

Calories: 80
Fat: 0g
Sodium: 0mg
Carbs: 20.5g
Sugar: 17.5g
Protein: 0.5g

Blueberry Crinkle

SLOW COOKER

Phyllis Good, Lancaster, PA

Makes 6–8 servings
Prep. Time: 15–20 minutes ⚬ Cooking Time: 2–3 hours ⚬ Ideal slow-cooker size: 3- or 4-qt.

⅓ cup turbinado sugar

¾ cup gluten-free oats

½ cup gluten-free flour

½ tsp. cinnamon

Dash of kosher salt

6 Tbsp. coconut oil, cold

4 cups blueberries, fresh or frozen

2 Tbsp. maple syrup

2 Tbsp. instant tapioca

2 Tbsp. lemon juice

½ tsp. lemon zest

1. Grease interior of slow cooker crock.

2. In a large bowl, combine turbinado sugar, oats, gluten-free flour, cinnamon, and salt.

3. Using two knives, a pastry cutter, or your fingers, work coconut oil into dry ingredients until small crumbs form.

4. In a separate bowl, stir together blueberries, maple syrup, tapioca, lemon juice, and lemon zest.

5. Spoon blueberry mixture into slow cooker crock.

6. Sprinkle crumbs over blueberries.

7. Cover. Cook 2–3 hours on Low, or until firm in the middle with juice bubbling up around the edges.

8. Remove lid with a giant swoop away from yourself so condensation on inside of lid doesn't drip on the crumbs.

9. Lift crock out of cooker. Let cool until either warm or room temperature before eating.

Calories: 280
Fat: 12.5g
Sodium: 25mg
Carbs: 40.5g
Sugar: 21.5g
Protein: 2.8g

Nectarine Almond Crisp

Hope Comerford, Clinton Township, MI

Makes 8–9 servings

Prep. Time: 10 minutes ⚬ *Cooking Time: 2 hours* ⚬ *Ideal slow-cooker size: 3- or 4-qt.*

5 nectarines, cored and sliced

¼ cup slivered almonds

1 tsp. cinnamon

¼ tsp. nutmeg

¼ tsp. ginger

1 tsp. vanilla extract

Crumble:

1 cup gluten-free oats

½ cup almond flour

½ cup slivered almonds

1 tsp. cinnamon

¼ tsp. ginger

½ tsp. sea salt

2 Tbsp. honey

2 Tbsp. coconut oil, melted

2–3 Tbsp. unsweetened almond milk

1. Spray crock with nonstick spray.

2. In the crock, combine nectarines, almonds, cinnamon, nutmeg, ginger, and vanilla.

3. In a medium bowl, combine all the crumble ingredients. If the mixture is too dry, add a bit more honey or almond milk. Pour over the top of the nectarine mixture.

4. Cover and cook on Low for 2 hours.

Serving suggestion:
Serve over frozen vanilla Greek yogurt.

Calories: 210
Fat: 10g
Sodium: 80mg
Carbs: 24.5g
Sugar: 13g
Protein: 5g

Healthy Coconut Apple Crisp

Hope Comerford, Clinton Township, MI

Makes 8–9 servings
Prep. Time: 20 minutes & Cooking Time: 2 hours & Ideal slow-cooker size: 3- or 4-qt.

5 medium Granny Smith apples, peeled, cored, sliced

1 Tbsp. cinnamon

¼ tsp. nutmeg

1 tsp. vanilla extract

Crumble:

1 cup gluten-free oats

½ cup coconut flour

½ cup unsweetened coconut flakes

1 tsp. cinnamon

⅛ tsp. nutmeg

½ tsp. sea salt

2 Tbsp. honey

2 Tbsp. coconut oil, melted

2–3 Tbsp. unsweetened coconut milk

1. Spray crock with nonstick spray

2. In the crock, combine apple slices, cinnamon, nutmeg, and vanilla.

3. In a medium bowl, combine all of the crumble ingredients. If too dry, add a bit more honey or coconut milk. Pour over top of apple mixture.

4. Cover slow cooker and cook on Low for 2 hours.

Serving suggestion:

Serve with a scoop of coconut ice cream.

Calories: 240
Fat: 8.5g
Sodium: 230mg
Carbs: 38.5g
Sugar: 18.5g
Protein: 5g

Quick Yummy Peaches

Willard E. Roth, Elkhart, IN

Makes 6 servings
Prep. Time: 5–20 minutes ♣ Cooking Time: 5 hours ♣ Ideal slow-cooker size: 3-qt.

⅓ cup low-fat gluten-free baking mix
⅔ cup gluten-free oats
⅓ cup maple syrup
1 tsp. ground cinnamon
4 cups sliced fresh peaches
½ cup water

1. Mix together baking mix, oats, maple syrup, and cinnamon in greased slow cooker.

2. Stir in peaches and water.

3. Cook on Low for at least 5 hours. (If you like a drier cobbler, remove lid for last 15–30 minutes of cooking.)

Calories: 140
Fat: 1g
Sodium: 60mg
Carbs: 33g
Sugar: 20g
Protein: 2g

Strawberry Mint Apple Crisp

SLOW COOKER

Hope Comerford, Clinton Township, MI

Makes 4 servings
Prep. Time: 20 minutes ⚭ Cooking Time: 2 hours ⚭ Ideal slow-cooker size: 2- or 3-qt.

2½–3 cups sliced strawberries

1 tsp. cinnamon

½ tsp. mint extract

1 tsp. vanilla extract

3 Tbsp. fresh chopped mint

Crumble:

½ cup gluten-free oats

¼ cup gluten-free oat flour

½ tsp. cinnamon

¼ tsp. salt

1 Tbsp. honey

1 Tbsp. coconut oil, melted

1–2 Tbsp. unsweetened almond or coconut milk

1. Spray crock with nonstick spray.

2. In the crock, combine strawberries, cinnamon, mint extract, vanilla extract, and fresh chopped mint.

3. In a bowl, combine all the crumble ingredients. If it's too dry, add a bit more honey or milk of your choice. Pour this mixture into the crock.

4. Cover and cook on Low for 2 hours.

Serving suggestion:
Serve with vanilla Greek yogurt.

Calories: 200
Fat: 6.5g
Sodium: 150mg
Carbs: 31.5g
Sugar: 10.5g
Protein: 5g

SLOW
COOKER

Tropical Fruit

Hope Comerford, Clinton Township, MI

Makes 14 servings
Prep. Time: 15 minutes ⚬ *Cooking Time: 3½–4 hours* ⚬ *Ideal slow-cooker size: 3- or 4-qt.*

24 oz. frozen mango, thawed, drained, and cut into 1-inch pieces

20-oz. can pineapple chunks, drained

16 oz. frozen peach slices, unsweetened

12-oz. pkg. soft coconut macaroon cookies, crumbled

½ cup dried cherries

¼ cup maple syrup

¼ cup melted coconut oil

1 tsp. lemon zest

2 Tbsp. lemon juice

1. Spray crock with nonstick spray.

2. Combine mango, pineapple, peaches, crumbled macaroons, and cherries in crock.

3. In a bowl, mix together the maple syrup, coconut oil, lemon zest, and lemon juice; pour over mixture in slow cooker.

4. Cover and cook on Low for 3½–4 hours.

Calories: 240
Fat: 10g
Sodium: 60mg
Carbs: 39g
Sugar: 31.5g
Protein: 1.5g

Homestyle Bread Pudding

SLOW COOKER

Lizzie Weaver, Ephrata, PA

Makes 6 servings
Prep. Time: 10–15 minutes ⚬ *Cooking Time: 2–3 hours*
Ideal slow-cooker size: large enough to hold your baking insert

⅓ cup Egg Beaters®

2¼ cups fat-free milk

½ tsp. ground cinnamon

¼ tsp. salt

⅓ cup maple syrup

1 tsp. vanilla extract

2 cups 1-inch bread cubes

½ cup raisins

1. Combine all ingredients in bowl. Pour into slow-cooker baking insert. Cover baking insert. Place on metal rack (or jar rings) in bottom of slow cooker.

2. Pour ½ cup hot water into cooker around outside of insert.

3. Cover slow cooker. Cook on High 2–3 hours.

4. Serve pudding warm or cold.

Calories: 150
Fat: 0.5g
Sodium: 230mg
Carbs: 32g
Sugar: 23g
Protein: 6g

Coconut Rice Pudding

Hope Comerford, Clinton Township, MI

Makes 6 servings
Prep. Time: 2 minutes 🔗 Cooking Time: 10 minutes

1 cup arborio rice, rinsed

1 cup unsweetened almond milk

14-oz. can light coconut milk

½ cup water

½ cup turbinado sugar, or sugar of your choice

1 stick cinnamon

¼ cup dried cranberries, *optional*

¼ cup unsweetened coconut flakes, *optional*

1. Place the rice into the inner pot of the Instant Pot, along with all the remaining ingredients.

2. Secure the lid and set the vent to sealing.

3. Using the Porridge setting, set the cook time for 10 minutes.

4. When the cooking time is over, let the pressure release naturally.

5. When the pin drops, remove the lid and remove cinnamon stick.

6. Stir and serve as is or sprinkle some cranberries and unsweetened coconut flakes on top of each serving. Enjoy!

Calories: 354
Fat: 6g
Sodium: 87mg
Carbs: 74g
Sugar: 43g
Protein: 4g

INSTANT
POT

Tapioca Pudding

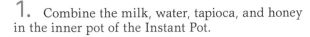

Nancy W. Huber, Green Park, PA

Makes 12 servings
Prep. Time: 5 minutes ⚜ *Cooking Time: 15 minutes* ⚜ *Cooling Time: 4 hours*

3 cups fat-free milk

I cup water

I cup small pearl tapioca

½ cup honey

4 eggs, beaten

I tsp. vanilla extract

1. Combine the milk, water, tapioca, and honey in the inner pot of the Instant Pot.

2. Secure the lid and set the vent to sealing.

3. Manually set the cook time for 6 minutes on high pressure.

4. When the cooking time is over, let the pressure release naturally for 10 minutes, then release any remaining pressure manually.

5. When the pin drops, remove the lid. Press Cancel.

6. Press the Sauté button.

7. In a bowl, mix the eggs and vanilla. Remove about ½ cup of the pudding from the inner pot and mix vigorously with the egg/vanilla mixture to temper the eggs. Then, add this mixture back to the rest of the pudding slowly, stirring. When it comes to a boil, press Cancel and remove the inner pot from the Instant Pot.

8. Let the pudding cool down to room temperature, then chill it for at least 4 hours.

Calories: 134
Fat: 2g
Sodium: 5mg
Carbs: 23g
Sugar: 15g
Protein: 4g

Metric Equivalent Measurements

If you're accustomed to using metric measurements, I don't want you to be inconvenienced by the imperial measurements I use in this book.

Use this handy chart, too, to figure out the size of the slow cooker you'll need for each recipe.

Weight (Dry Ingredients)

1 oz		30 g
4 oz	¼ lb	120 g
8 oz	½ lb	240 g
12 oz	¾ lb	360 g
16 oz	1 lb	480 g
32 oz	2 lb	960 g

Slow-Cooker Sizes

1-quart	0.96 l
2-quart	1.92 l
3-quart	2.88 l
4-quart	3.84 l
5-quart	4.80 l
6-quart	5.76 l
7-quart	6.72 l
8-quart	7.68 l

Volume (Liquid Ingredients)

½ tsp.		2 ml
1 tsp.		5 ml
1 Tbsp.	½ fl oz	15 ml
2 Tbsp.	1 fl oz	30 ml
¼ cup	2 fl oz	60 ml
⅓ cup	3 fl oz	80 ml
½ cup	4 fl oz	120 ml
⅔ cup	5 fl oz	160 ml
¾ cup	6 fl oz	180 ml
1 cup	8 fl oz	240 ml
1 pt	16 fl oz	480 ml
1 qt	32 fl oz	960 ml

Length

¼ in	6 mm
½ in	13 mm
¾ in	19 mm
1 in	25 mm
6 in	15 cm
12 in	30 cm

Recipe & Ingredient Index

A

almonds
Best Steel-Cut Oats, 38
Nectarine Almond Crisp, 195
Quinoa with Almonds and
Cranberries, 157
Spiced Lentils with Chicken
and Rice, 99
Steak and Rice Dinner, 124
apple
Healthy Coconut Apple Crisp,
196
Korean-Inspired BBQ
Shredded Pork, 111
Red Wine Apple Roast, 117
applesauce
Applesauce Pork Chops with
Sweet Potatoes, 107
Giant Healthy Pancake, 29
Zucchini Chocolate Chip
Bars, 189
Applesauce Pork Chops with
Sweet Potatoes, 107
artichoke hearts
Spinach Artichoke Dip, 19
Artichokes and Brown Rice, 159
Artichoke-Tomato Chicken, 83
Asian-Style Chicken with
Pineapple, 91
asparagus
Lemony Garlic Asparagus, 183
Aunt Twila's Beans, 173

B

Baked Ziti, 138
Bananas Foster, 191
basil
Brussels Sprouts with
Pimentos, 179
Chicken and Vegetable Soup, 47
Chicken Dinner in a Packet, 89
Easy Enchilada Shredded
Chicken, 93

Garlic Galore Rotisserie
Chicken, 80
Herbed Fish Fillets, 150
Italian Frittata, 35
Meat Sauce for Spaghetti, 120
Raspberry Balsamic Pork
Chops, 104
Savory Rice, 163
Slow-Cooker Tomato Soup, 53
Turkey Sausage and Cabbage
Soup, 49
bay leaf
Quinoa with Almonds and
Cranberries, 157
Sweet Potato Soup with Kale,
59
beans
black
Black Bean Brownies, 188
Black Bean Soup with
Fresh Salsa, 57
Pumpkin Chili, 66
cannellini
Italian Shredded Pork Stew,
62
garbanzo
Chicken Chickpea Tortilla
Soup, 46
Italian Crockpot Chicken, 79
White Chili, 67
great northern
White and Green Chili, 69
White Beans with Sun-
Dried Tomatoes, 171
green
Greek-Style Green Beans,
182
Honey Balsamic Chicken, 85
kidney
Pumpkin Chili, 66
Veggie Minestrone, 51
navy
White Chili, 67

pinto
Aunt Twila's Beans, 173
White Chili, 67
refried
Seven Layer Dip, 18
white
Italian Shredded Pork Stew,
62
White Bean Soup, 55
beef
chuck roast
Beef with Broccoli, 121
Colorful Beef Stew, 65
Hungarian Beef with
Paprika, 115
eye of round
Spicy Beef Roast, 119
ground
Beef and Zucchini
Casserole, 123
roast
Low-Fat Slow-Cooker
Roast, 116
Red Wine Apple Roast, 117
round steak
Slow-Cooker Swiss Steak,
125
Steak and Rice Dinner, 124
Beef and Zucchini Casserole, 123
Beef with Broccoli, 121
beets
Slow-Cooker Beets, 175
bell pepper
Broccoli and Bell Peppers, 181
Chicken Chili Pepper Stew, 61
Colorful Beef Stew, 65
Enchilada Soup, 54
Fiesta Hashbrowns, 30
Hometown Spanish Rice, 162
Hot Tuna Macaroni Casserole,
154
Hungarian Beef with Paprika,
115

Lentils with Cheese, 141
Pumpkin Chili, 66
Quinoa with Vegetables, 158
Rosemary Carrots, 178
Slim Dunk, 17
Vegetarian Sausage and Sweet
 Pepper Hash, 30
White Bean Soup, 55
White Chili, 67
Best Steel-Cut Oats, 38
Black Bean Brownies, 188
Black Bean Soup with Fresh
 Salsa, 57
blueberries
Blueberry Crinkle, 193
Blueberry Crinkle, 193
bread
Breakfast Sausage Casserole,
 33
Homestyle Bread Pudding, 201
breakfast
Best Steel-Cut Oats, 38
Breakfast Sausage Casserole,
 33
Fiesta Hashbrowns, 30
Giant Healthy Pancake, 29
Grain and Fruit Cereal, 42
Insta-Oatmeal, 39
Italian Frittata, 35
Oatmeal Morning, 41
Pumpkin Breakfast Custard, 37
Spinach Frittata, 34
Vegetarian Sausage and Sweet
 Pepper Hash, 31
Breakfast Sausage Casserole, 33
broccoli
Beef with Broccoli, 121
Juicy Orange Chicken, 92
Broccoli and Bell Peppers, 181
Brown Sugar Pork Chops, 105
Brussels Sprouts with Pimentos,
 179

C
cabbage
Turkey Sausage and Cabbage
 Soup, 49

Unstuffed Cabbage Soup, 50
Cajun Catfish, 153
caraway
Hungarian Beef with Paprika,
 115
cardamom
Dates in Cardamom Coffee
 Syrup, 192
Spiced Lentils with Chicken
 and Rice, 99
Carnitas, 112
carrots
Chicken and Vegetable Soup,
 47
Chicken Chili Pepper Stew, 61
Chicken Dinner in a Packet,
 89
Chicken Rice Bake, 96
Lentils with Cheese, 141
Low-Fat Slow-Cooker Roast,
 116
Mediterranean Lentil Soup, 58
Moroccan Spiced Stew, 63
Poached Chicken, 87
Quinoa with Vegetables, 158
Slow-Cooker Swiss Steak, 125
Steak and Rice Dinner, 124
Turkey Sausage and Cabbage
 Soup, 49
Veggie Minestrone, 51
catfish
Cajun Catfish, 153
cauliflower
Faked-You-Out Alfredo, 139
Hot Tuna Macaroni Casserole,
 154
cayenne
Cajun Catfish, 153
Moroccan Spiced Stew, 63
cereal
Cranberry Almond Coconut
 Snack Mix, 23
Gluten-Free Chex Mix, 22
Cheerios
Cranberry Almond Coconut
 Snack Mix, 23
Gluten-Free Chex Mix, 22

cheese
cheddar
Breakfast Sausage
 Casserole, 33
Lentils with Cheese, 141
Mexi Rotini, 137
cottage
Black Bean Brownies, 188
Spinach Pie, 133
cream
Spinach Artichoke Dip, 19
Mediterranean Lentil Soup,
 58
Mexican blend
Seven Layer Dip, 18
Monterey Jack
Double Corn Tortilla Bake,
 135
Fiesta Hashbrowns, 30
mozzarella
Baked Ziti, 138
Spinach Pie, 133
Turkey "Spaghetti" Quinoa,
 100
Parmesan
Beef and Zucchini
 Casserole, 123
Hometown Spanish Rice,
 162
Italian Frittata, 35
Mushroom Risotto, 129
Spinach Artichoke Dip, 19
Spinach Frittata, 34
Spinach Pie, 133
Veggie Minestrone, 51
White Beans with Sun-
 Dried Tomatoes, 171
cherries
dried
Best Steel-Cut Oats, 38
Quinoa with Almonds and
 Cranberries, 157
Tropical Fruit, 200
Chex
Gluten-Free Chex Mix, 22
chicken
breast

Artichoke-Tomato Chicken, 83

Asian-Style Chicken with Pineapple, 91

Chicken Chickpea Tortilla Soup, 46

Chicken Chili Pepper Stew, 61

Chicken Dinner in a Packet, 89

Chicken Rice Bake, 96

Chicken Tortilla Soup, 45

Easy Enchilada Shredded Chicken, 93

Garlic and Lemon Chicken, 75

Italian Crockpot Chicken, 79

Juicy Orange Chicken, 92

Lemon and Olive Oil Chicken, 76

Southwestern Shredded Chicken, 95

Spiced Lentils with Chicken and Rice, 99

Chicken and Vegetable Soup, 47

Garlic Galore Rotisserie Chicken, 80

ground
   Chicken Lettuce Wraps, 21

Poached Chicken, 87

thighs
   Chicken Curry with Rice, 97
   Garlic and Lemon Chicken, 75
   Honey Balsamic Chicken, 85
   Lemon and Olive Oil Chicken, 76
   Lemony Chicken Thighs, 77
   Spanish Chicken, 88

Chicken and Vegetable Soup, 47

Chicken Chickpea Tortilla Soup, 46

Chicken Chili Pepper Stew, 61

Chicken Curry with Rice, 97

Chicken Dinner in a Packet, 89

Chicken Lettuce Wraps, 21

Chicken Rice Bake, 96

Chicken Tortilla Soup, 45

chili
   Pumpkin Chili, 66
   White and Green Chili, 69
   White Chili, 67

chili powder
   Black Bean Soup with Fresh Salsa, 57
   Easy Enchilada Shredded Chicken, 93
   Garlic Galore Rotisserie Chicken, 80
   Korean-Inspired BBQ Shredded Pork, 111
   Maple-Glazed Salmon, 146
   Pumpkin Chili, 66
   Seven Layer Dip, 18
   Southwestern Shredded Chicken, 95

chili sauce
   Spicy Orange Tofu, 134

chocolate
   Fudgy Secret Brownies, 187

chocolate chips
   Zucchini Chocolate Chip Bars, 189

cilantro
   Black Bean Soup with Fresh Salsa, 57
   Chicken Chickpea Tortilla Soup, 46
   Chicken Chili Pepper Stew, 61
   Quinoa with Vegetables, 158
   Spiced Lentils with Chicken and Rice, 99
   White and Green Chili, 69

Cilantro Lime Rice, 161

cinnamon
   Bananas Foster, 191
   Best Steel-Cut Oats, 38
   Blueberry Crinkle, 193
   Cranberry Almond Coconut Snack Mix, 23

Dates in Cardamom Coffee Syrup, 192

Grain and Fruit Cereal, 42

Greek-Style Green Beans, 182

Healthy Coconut Apple Crisp, 196

Homestyle Bread Pudding, 201

Insta-Oatmeal, 39

Moroccan Spiced Stew, 63

Nectarine Almond Crisp, 195

Oatmeal Morning, 41

Pumpkin Breakfast Custard, 37

Quick Yummy Peaches, 197

Quinoa with Almonds and Cranberries, 157

Spanish Chicken, 88

Spiced Lentils with Chicken and Rice, 99

Strawberry Mint Apple Crisp, 199

Sweet Potato Puree, 170

Zucchini Chocolate Chip Bars, 189

cloves
   Pumpkin Breakfast Custard, 37
   White Bean Soup, 55

cocoa
   Black Bean Brownies, 188

coconut
   Cranberry Almond Coconut Snack Mix, 23
   Healthy Coconut Apple Crisp, 196

Coconut Rice Pudding, 203

cod
   Spiced Cod, 151

coffee
   Dates in Cardamom Coffee Syrup, 192

Colorful Beef Stew, 65

cookies
   macaroon
      Tropical Fruit, 200

coriander
   Sweet Potato Soup with Kale, 59

corn
    Chicken Chili Pepper Stew, 61
    Chicken Tortilla Soup, 45
    Double Corn Tortilla Bake, 135
    Enchilada Soup, 54
Corn on the Cob, 177
cranberries
    dried
        Cranberry Almond
            Coconut Snack Mix, 23
        Grain and Fruit Cereal, 42
        Oatmeal Morning, 41
        Quinoa with Almonds and
            Cranberries, 157
Cranberry Almond Coconut
    Snack Mix, 23
cumin
    Aunt Twila's Beans, 173
    Black Bean Soup with Fresh
        Salsa, 57
    Carnitas, 112
    Chicken Chickpea Tortilla
        Soup, 46
    Chicken Chili Pepper Stew, 61
    Garlic Galore Rotisserie
        Chicken, 80
    Maple-Glazed Salmon, 146
    Moroccan Spiced Stew, 63
    Pumpkin Chili, 66
    Southwestern Shredded
        Chicken, 95
    Spiced Cod, 151
    Spiced Lentils with Chicken
        and Rice, 99
    White and Green Chili, 69
    White Chili, 67
curry powder
    Chicken Curry with Rice, 97
custard
    Pumpkin Breakfast Custard, 37

D
Dates in Cardamom Coffee
    Syrup, 192
desserts
    Bananas Foster, 191

    Black Bean Brownies, 188
    Blueberry Crinkle, 193
    Coconut Rice Pudding, 203
    Dates in Cardamom Coffee
        Syrup, 192
    Fudgy Secret Brownies, 187
    Healthy Coconut Apple Crisp,
        196
    Homestyle Bread Pudding,
        201
    Nectarine Almond Crisp, 195
    Quick Yummy Peaches, 197
    Strawberry Mint Apple Crisp,
        199
    Tapioca Pudding, 204
    Tropical Fruit, 200
    Zucchini Chocolate Chip
        Bars, 189
dill
    Herbed Fish Fillets, 150
    Quinoa with Spinach, 130
dip
    Seven Layer Dip, 18
    Spinach Artichoke Dip, 19
Double Corn Tortilla Bake, 135

E
Easy Enchilada Shredded
    Chicken, 93
eggs
    Double Corn Tortilla Bake,
        135
    Italian Frittata, 35
    Spinach Frittata, 34
enchilada sauce
    Easy Enchilada Shredded
        Chicken, 93
    Enchilada Soup, 54
Enchilada Soup, 54

F
Faked-You-Out Alfredo, 139
Fiesta Hashbrowns, 30
frittata
    Italian Frittata, 35
Fudgy Secret Brownies, 187

G
garlic
    Artichoke-Tomato Chicken,
        83
    Aunt Twila's Beans, 173
    Beef with Broccoli, 121
    Black Bean Soup with Fresh
        Salsa, 57
    Carnitas, 112
    Chicken and Vegetable Soup,
        47
    Chicken Chickpea Tortilla
        Soup, 46
    Chicken Lettuce Wraps, 21
    Chicken Rice Bake, 96
    Chicken Tortilla Soup, 45
    Colorful Beef Stew, 65
    Faked-You-Out Alfredo, 139
    Garlic and Lemon Chicken,
        75
    Garlic Galore Rotisserie
        Chicken, 80
    Ginger Pork Chops, 103
    Honey Balsamic Chicken, 85
    Honey Lemon Garlic Salmon,
        147
    Hungarian Beef with Paprika,
        115
    Italian Shredded Pork Stew,
        62
    Korean-Inspired BBQ
        Shredded Pork, 111
    Lemon and Olive Oil
        Chicken, 76
    Lemony Chicken Thighs, 77
    Lemony Garlic Asparagus,
        183
    Lentils with Cheese, 141
    Moist and Tender Turkey
        Breast, 84
    Mushroom Risotto, 129
    Potatoes with Parsley, 174
    Quick and Light Sweet Potato
        Wedges, 169
    Quinoa with Vegetables, 158

Red Wine Apple Roast, 117
Slow-Cooker Tomato Soup, 53
Spiced Lentils with Chicken and Rice, 99
Spicy Beef Roast, 119
Spicy Orange Tofu, 134
Spinach Artichoke Dip, 19
Sweet Potato Soup with Kale, 59
Thyme and Garlic Turkey Breast, 81
Thyme Roasted Sweet Potatoes, 167
Turkey Sausage and Cabbage Soup, 49
Unstuffed Cabbage Soup, 50
Veggie Minestrone, 51
White Beans with Sun-Dried Tomatoes, 171
White Chili, 67
Garlic and Lemon Chicken, 75
Garlic Galore Rotisserie Chicken, 80
garlic powder
    Baked Ziti, 138
    Beef and Zucchini Casserole, 123
    Brown Sugar Pork Chops, 105
    Easy Enchilada Shredded Chicken, 93
    Garlic Galore Rotisserie Chicken, 80
    Gluten-Free Chex Mix, 22
    Low-Fat Slow-Cooker Roast, 116
    Pumpkin Chili, 66
    Raspberry Balsamic Pork Chops, 104
    Savory Rice, 163
    Slow-Cooker Swiss Steak, 125
    Southwestern Shredded Chicken, 95
    Spanish Chicken, 88
    Spiced Cod, 151
    Turkey "Spaghetti" Quinoa, 100
Giant Healthy Pancake, 29

ginger
    Asian-Style Chicken with Pineapple, 91
    Ginger Pork Chops, 103
    Korean-Inspired BBQ Shredded Pork, 111
    Moroccan Spiced Stew, 63
    Nectarine Almond Crisp, 195
    Pumpkin Breakfast Custard, 37
    Spicy Orange Tofu, 134
Ginger Pork Chops, 103
Gluten-Free Chex Mix, 22
Grain and Fruit Cereal, 42
Greek-Style Green Beans, 182
green chilies
    Chicken Chickpea Tortilla Soup, 46
    Double Corn Tortilla Bake, 135
    Enchilada Soup, 54
    Mexi Rotini, 137
    Seven Layer Dip, 18
    Southwestern Shredded Chicken, 95
    White and Green Chili, 69

H
hashbrowns
    Fiesta Hashbrowns, 30
Healthy Coconut Apple Crisp, 196
Herbed Fish Fillets, 150
Homestyle Bread Pudding, 201
Hometown Spanish Rice, 162
honey
    Cranberry Almond Coconut Snack Mix, 23
Honey Balsamic Chicken, 85
Honey Lemon Garlic Salmon, 147
Honey Nut Cheerios
    Cranberry Almond Coconut Snack Mix, 23
hot sauce
    Korean-Inspired BBQ Shredded Pork, 111
Hot Tuna Macaroni Casserole, 154

Hungarian Beef with Paprika, 115

I
instant pot
    Artichokes and Brown Rice, 159
    Beef and Zucchini Casserole, 123
    Best Steel-Cut Oats, 38
    Black Bean Soup with Fresh Salsa, 57
    Chicken Chili Pepper Stew, 61
    Chicken Dinner in a Packet, 89
    Chicken Rice Bake, 96
    Cilantro Lime Rice, 161
    Coconut Rice Pudding, 203
    Garlic Galore Rotisserie Chicken, 80
    Giant Healthy Pancake, 29
    Ginger Pork Chops, 103
    Herbed Fish Fillets, 150
    Hometown Spanish Rice, 162
    Honey Lemon Garlic Salmon, 147
    Instant Spaghetti Squash, 165
    Insta-Oatmeal, 39
    Insta-Popcorn, 25
    Lemon and Olive Oil Chicken, 76
    Lemon Pepper Tilapia, 149
    Lemony Chicken Thighs, 77
    Lentils with Cheese, 141
    Maple-Glazed Salmon, 146
    Mushroom Risotto, 129
    Perfect Sweet Potatoes, 166
    Potatoes with Parsley, 174
    Quinoa with Almonds and Cranberries, 157
    Quinoa with Spinach, 130
    Rosemary Carrots, 178
    Simple Salmon, 145
    Spiced Lentils with Chicken and Rice, 99
    Spinach Artichoke Dip, 19
    Spinach Pie, 133

Spinach Stuffed Tomatoes, 131
Sweet Potato Puree, 170
Sweet Potato Soup with Kale, 59
Tapioca Pudding, 204
Turkey Sausage and Cabbage Soup, 49
Unstuffed Cabbage Soup, 50
Veggie Minestrone, 51
White Bean Soup, 55
Instant Spaghetti Squash, 165
Insta-Oatmeal, 39
Insta-Popcorn, 25
Italian Crockpot Chicken, 79
Italian dressing
Quick and Light Sweet Potato Wedges, 169
Italian Frittata, 35
Italian seasoning
Baked Ziti, 138
Quick and Light Sweet Potato Wedges, 169
Italian Shredded Pork Stew, 62

J
jalapeño
Chicken Chili Pepper Stew, 61
Chicken Tortilla Soup, 45
Juicy Orange Chicken, 92

K
kale
Italian Shredded Pork Stew, 62
Sweet Potato Soup with Kale, 59
ketchup
Korean Inspired BBQ Shredded Pork, 111
White Bean Soup, 55
Korean-Inspired BBQ Shredded Pork, 111

L
lamb
Moroccan Spiced Stew, 63
leek soup mix
Slim Dunk, 17

Lemon and Olive Oil Chicken, 76
Lemon Pepper Tilapia, 149
Lemony Chicken Thighs, 77
Lemony Garlic Asparagus, 183
lentils
Mediterranean Lentil Soup, 58
Spiced Lentils with Chicken and Rice, 99
Lentils with Cheese, 141
lettuce
Chicken Lettuce Wraps, 21
liquid aminos
Asian-Style Chicken with Pineapple, 91
Broccoli and Bell Peppers, 181
Chicken Lettuce Wraps, 21
Juicy Orange Chicken, 92
Spicy Beef Roast, 119
Low-Fat Slow-Cooker Roast, 116

M
mango
Tropical Fruit, 200
Maple-Glazed Salmon, 146
maple syrup
Blueberry Crinkle, 193
Grain and Fruit Cereal, 42
Homestyle Bread Pudding, 201
Insta-Oatmeal, 39
Maple-Glazed Salmon, 146
Pumpkin Breakfast Custard, 37
Quick Yummy Peaches, 197
Tropical Fruit, 200
marjoram
Colorful Beef Stew, 65
Greek-Style Green Beans, 182
Lentils with Cheese, 141
Mediterranean Lentil Soup, 58
marmalade
Spicy Orange Tofu, 134
mayonnaise
Spinach Artichoke Dip, 19

meatless
Baked Ziti, 138
Double Corn Tortilla Bake, 135
Faked-You-Out Alfredo, 139
Lentils with Cheese, 141
Mexi Rotini, 137
Mushroom Risotto, 129
Quinoa with Spinach, 130
Spicy Orange Tofu, 134
Spinach Pie, 133
Spinach Stuffed Tomatoes, 131
meatless crumbles
Mexi Rotini, 137
Unstuffed Cabbage Soup, 50
White and Green Chili, 69
Meat Sauce for Spaghetti, 120
Mediterranean Lentil Soup, 58
Mexi Rotini, 137
millet
Grain and Fruit Cereal, 42
mint
Italian Frittata, 35
Strawberry Mint Apple Crisp, 199
Miracle Whip
Slim Dunk, 17
Moist and Tender Turkey Breast, 84
molasses
Pumpkin Breakfast Custard, 37
White Bean Soup, 55
Moroccan Spiced Stew, 63
Mushroom Risotto, 129
mushrooms
Beef and Zucchini Casserole, 123
Chicken and Vegetable Soup, 47
Chicken Dinner in a Packet, 89
Chicken Rice Bake, 96
Fiesta Hashbrowns, 30
Hot Tuna Macaroni Casserole, 154

Italian Crockpot Chicken, 79
Steak and Rice Dinner, 124
mustard
    Brown Sugar Pork Chops, 105
    dry
        Spicy Beef Roast, 119

N
Nectarine Almond Crisp, 195
noodles
    Baked Ziti, 138
    Faked-You-Out Alfredo, 139
    Hot Tuna Macaroni Casserole,
        154
    Mexi Rotini, 137
    Veggie Minestrone, 51
nutmeg
    Bananas Foster, 191
    Greek-Style Green Beans, 182
    Healthy Coconut Apple Crisp,
        196
    Nectarine Almond Crisp, 195
    Pumpkin Breakfast Custard, 37
    Sweet Potato Puree, 170

O
Oatmeal Morning, 41
oats
    Best Steel-Cut Oats, 38
    Blueberry Crinkle, 193
    Cranberry Almond Coconut
        Snack Mix, 23
    Healthy Coconut Apple Crisp,
        196
    Insta-Oatmeal, 39
    Nectarine Almond Crisp, 195
    Quick Yummy Peaches, 197
    Strawberry Mint Apple Crisp,
        199
okra
    Fudgy Secret Brownies, 187
Old Bay seasoning
    Simple Salmon, 145
olives
    black
        Brussels Sprouts with
            Pimentos, 179

Seven Layer Dip, 18
White Beans with Sun-
    Dried Tomatoes, 171
onion powder
    Asian-Style Chicken with
        Pineapple, 91
    Baked Ziti, 138
    Garlic Galore Rotisserie
        Chicken, 80
    Gluten-Free Chex Mix, 22
    Southwestern Shredded
        Chicken, 95
    Spiced Cod, 151
    Spinach Artichoke Dip, 19
    Thyme and Garlic Turkey
        Breast, 81
orange juice
    Juicy Orange Chicken, 92
    Thyme and Garlic Turkey
        Breast, 81
oregano
    Beef and Zucchini Casserole, 123
    Black Bean Soup with Fresh
        Salsa, 57
    Brussels Sprouts with
        Pimentos, 179
    Cajun Catfish, 153
    Carnitas, 112
    Chicken Tortilla Soup, 45
    Greek-Style Green Beans, 182
    Italian Frittata, 35
    Lemony Chicken Thighs, 77
    Meat Sauce for Spaghetti, 120
    Spinach Pie, 133
    Turkey Sausage and Cabbage
        Soup, 49
    Unstuffed Cabbage Soup, 50
    Veggie Minestrone, 51
    White Chili, 67

P
pancake
    Giant Healthy Pancake, 29
paprika
    Cajun Catfish, 153
    Chicken Chickpea Tortilla
        Soup, 46

Colorful Beef Stew, 65
Hungarian Beef with Paprika,
    115
Lemon and Olive Oil
    Chicken, 76
Maple-Glazed Salmon, 146
Sweet Potato Soup with Kale,
    59
parsley
    Cajun Catfish, 153
    Herbed Fish Fillets, 150
    Honey Lemon Garlic Salmon,
        147
    Hungarian Beef with Paprika,
        115
    Lemon and Olive Oil
        Chicken, 76
    Lemony Chicken Thighs, 77
    Mediterranean Lentil Soup,
        58
    Potatoes with Parsley, 174
    Savory Rice, 163
    Unstuffed Cabbage Soup, 50
    Vegetarian Sausage and Sweet
        Pepper Hash, 30
peaches
    Quick Yummy Peaches, 197
    Tropical Fruit, 200
peanut butter
    Chicken Lettuce Wraps, 21
peanuts
    Gluten-Free Chex Mix, 22
peas
    frozen
        Mushroom Risotto, 129
pecans
    Fudgy Secret Brownies, 187
Perfect Sweet Potatoes, 166
pimentos
    Brussels Sprouts with
        Pimentos, 179
pineapple
    Asian-Style Chicken with
        Pineapple, 91
    Brown Sugar Pork Chops, 105
    Tropical Fruit, 200
    Tropical Pork with Yams, 108

Poached Chicken, 87
popcorn
    Insta-Popcorn, 25
pork
    butt
        Italian Shredded Pork Stew,
           62
    chops
        Applesauce Pork Chops
           with Sweet Potatoes, 107
        Brown Sugar Pork Chops,
           105
        Ginger Pork Chops, 103
        Raspberry Balsamic Pork
           Chops, 104
    loin
        Pork and Sweet Potatoes, 109
        Tropical Pork with Yams, 108
    shoulder
        Carnitas, 112
        Italian Shredded Pork Stew,
           62
    sirloin tip roast
        Korean-Inspired BBQ
           Shredded Pork, 111
Pork and Sweet Potatoes, 109
potatoes
    Fiesta Hashbrowns, 30
    Low-Fat Slow-Cooker Roast,
        116
    red
        Honey Balsamic Chicken,
           85
        Potatoes with Parsley, 174
    Slow-Cooker Swiss Steak, 125
    sweet
        Applesauce Pork Chops
           with Sweet Potatoes, 107
        Italian Shredded Pork Stew,
           62
        Moroccan Spiced Stew, 63
        Perfect Sweet Potatoes, 166
        Pork and Sweet Potatoes,
           109
        Quick and Light Sweet
           Potato Wedges, 169
        Sweet Potato Puree, 170

Sweet Potato Soup with
    Kale, 59
Thyme Roasted Sweet
    Potatoes, 167
White Bean Soup, 55
Vegetarian Sausage and Sweet
    Pepper Hash, 30, 31
Potatoes with Parsley, 174
prosciutto
    Italian Frittata, 35
pudding
    Coconut Rice Pudding, 203
    Homestyle Bread Pudding, 201
    Tapioca Pudding, 204
Pumpkin Breakfast Custard, 37
Pumpkin Chili, 66

Q

Quick and Light Sweet Potato
    Wedges, 169
Quick Yummy Peaches, 197
quinoa
    Enchilada Soup, 54
    Grain and Fruit Cereal, 42
    Turkey "Spaghetti" Quinoa,
        100
Quinoa with Almonds and
    Cranberries, 157
Quinoa with Spinach, 130
Quinoa with Vegetables, 158

R

raisins
    Best Steel-Cut Oats, 38
    Grain and Fruit Cereal, 42
    Homestyle Bread Pudding, 201
    Spiced Lentils with Chicken
        and Rice, 99
Raspberry Balsamic Pork Chops,
    104
Red Wine Apple Roast, 117
rice
    arborio
        Mushroom Risotto, 129
    brown
        Artichokes and Brown
           Rice, 159

Beef and Zucchini
    Casserole, 123
Chicken Curry with Rice,
    97
Chicken Rice Bake, 96
Grain and Fruit Cereal, 42
Savory Rice, 163
Spiced Lentils with
    Chicken and Rice, 99
Unstuffed Cabbage Soup,
    50
Cilantro Lime Rice, 161
Hometown Spanish Rice, 162
wild
    Steak and Rice Dinner, 124
rosemary
    Honey Balsamic Chicken, 85
    Sweet Potato Soup with Kale,
        59
Rosemary Carrots, 178

S

sage
    Italian Frittata, 35
    Lentils with Cheese, 141
salmon
    Honey Lemon Garlic Salmon,
        147
    Maple-Glazed Salmon, 146
    Simple Salmon, 145
salsa
    Black Bean Soup with Fresh
        Salsa, 57
    Seven Layer Dip, 18
salsa verde
    White and Green Chili, 69
sausage
    Italian
        Vegetarian Sausage and
           Sweet Pepper Hash, 31
    meatless crumbles
        Breakfast Sausage
           Casserole, 33
    turkey
        Fiesta Hashbrowns, 30
        Turkey Sausage and
           Cabbage Soup, 49

vegetarian Italian
Vegetarian Sausage and
Sweet Pepper Hash, 30
Savory Rice, 163
seafood
Cajun Catfish, 153
Herbed Fish Fillets, 150
Honey Lemon Garlic Salmon, 147
Hot Tuna Macaroni Casserole, 154
Lemon Pepper Tilapia, 149
Maple-Glazed Salmon, 146
Simple Salmon, 145
Spiced Cod, 151
sesame oil
Chicken Lettuce Wraps, 21
sesame seeds
Broccoli and Bell Peppers, 181
Seven Layer Dip, 18
sherry
Mediterranean Lentil Soup, 58
Simple Salmon, 145
Slim Dunk, 17
slow cooker
Applesauce Pork Chops with Sweet Potatoes, 107
Artichoke-Tomato Chicken, 83
Asian-Style Chicken with Pineapple, 91
Aunt Twila's Beans, 173
Baked Ziti, 138
Bananas Foster, 191
Beef with Broccoli, 121
Black Bean Brownies, 188
Blueberry Crinkle, 193
Breakfast Sausage Casserole, 33
Broccoli and Bell Peppers, 181
Brown Sugar Pork Chops, 105
Brussels Sprouts with Pimentos, 179
Cajun Catfish, 153
Carnitas, 112

Chicken and Vegetable Soup, 47
Chicken Chickpea Tortilla Soup, 46
Chicken Curry with Rice, 97
Chicken Lettuce Wraps, 21
Chicken Tortilla Soup, 45
Colorful Beef Stew, 65
Corn on the Cob, 177
Cranberry Almond Coconut Snack Mix, 23
Dates in Cardamom Coffee Syrup, 192
Double Corn Tortilla Bake, 135
Easy Enchilada Shredded Chicken, 93
Enchilada Soup, 54
Faked-You-Out Alfredo, 139
Fiesta Hashbrowns, 30
Fudgy Secret Brownies, 187
Garlic and Lemon Chicken, 75
Gluten-Free Chex Mix, 22
Grain and Fruit Cereal, 42
Greek-Style Green Beans, 182
Healthy Coconut Apple Crisp, 196
Homestyle Bread Pudding, 201
Honey Balsamic Chicken, 85
Hot Tuna Macaroni Casserole, 154
Hungarian Beef with Paprika, 115
Italian Crockpot Chicken, 79
Italian Frittata, 35
Italian Shredded Pork Stew, 62
Juicy Orange Chicken, 92
Korean-Inspired BBQ Shredded Pork, 111
Lemony Garlic Asparagus, 183
Low-Fat Slow-Cooker Roast, 116
Meat Sauce for Spaghetti, 120
Mexi Rotini, 137

Moist and Tender Turkey Breast, 84
Moroccan Spiced Stew, 63
Nectarine Almond Crisp, 195
Oatmeal Morning, 41
Poached Chicken, 87
Pork and Sweet Potatoes, 109
Pumpkin Breakfast Custard, 37
Pumpkin Chili, 66
Quick and Light Sweet Potato Wedges, 169
Quick Yummy Peaches, 197
Quinoa with Vegetables, 158
Raspberry Balsamic Pork Chops, 104
Red Wine Apple Roast, 117
Savory Rice, 163
Seven Layer Dip, 18
Slim Dunk, 17
Slow-Cooker Beets, 175
Slow-Cooker Swiss Steak, 125
Slow-Cooker Tomato Soup, 53
Southwestern Shredded Chicken, 95
Spanish Chicken, 88
Spiced Cod, 151
Spicy Beef Roast, 119
Spicy Orange Tofu, 134
Spinach Frittata, 34
Steak and Rice Dinner, 124
Strawberry Mint Apple Crisp, 199
Thyme and Garlic Turkey Breast, 81
Thyme Roasted Sweet Potatoes, 167
Tropical Fruit, 200
Tropical Pork with Yams, 108
Turkey "Spaghetti" Quinoa, 100
Vegetarian Sausage and Sweet Pepper Hash, 30, 31
White and Green Chili, 69
White Beans with Sun-Dried Tomatoes, 171
White Chili, 67

Zucchini Chocolate Chip
  Bars, 189
Slow-Cooker Beets, 175
Slow-Cooker Swiss Steak, 125
Slow-Cooker Tomato Soup, 53
soup. *See also* stew
  Chicken and Vegetable Soup,
    47
  Chicken Chickpea Tortilla
    Soup, 46
  Chicken Tortilla Soup, 45
  Enchilada Soup, 54
  Mediterranean Lentil Soup,
    58
  Slow-Cooker Tomato Soup, 53
  Sweet Potato Soup with Kale,
    59
  Turkey Sausage and Cabbage
    Soup, 49
  Unstuffed Cabbage Soup, 50
  Veggie Minestrone, 51
  White Bean Soup, 55
sour cream
  Black Bean Soup with Fresh
    Salsa, 57
  Italian Shredded Pork Stew,
    62
  Slim Dunk, 17
  Spinach Artichoke Dip, 19
Southwestern Shredded
  Chicken, 95
soy sauce
  Beef with Broccoli, 121
  Broccoli and Bell Peppers, 181
  Chicken Lettuce Wraps, 21
  Ginger Pork Chops, 103
  Korean-Inspired BBQ
    Shredded Pork, 111
  Spanish Chicken, 88
  Spicy Beef Roast, 119
  Tropical Pork with Yams, 108
Spanish Chicken, 88
Spiced Cod, 151
Spiced Lentils with Chicken and
  Rice, 99
Spicy Beef Roast, 119
Spicy Orange Tofu, 134

spinach
  Italian Crockpot Chicken, 79
  Quinoa with Spinach, 130
  Slim Dunk, 17
  Spinach Artichoke Dip, 19
  Spinach Frittata, 34
  Veggie Minestrone, 51
Spinach Artichoke Dip, 19
Spinach Frittata, 34
Spinach Pie, 133
Spinach Stuffed Tomatoes, 131
squash
  Instant Spaghetti Squash, 165
Steak and Rice Dinner, 124
stew. *See also* soup
  Chicken Chili Pepper Stew, 61
  Colorful Beef Stew, 65
  Italian Shredded Pork Stew,
    62
  Moroccan Spiced Stew, 63
strawberries
  Strawberry Mint Apple Crisp,
    199
Strawberry Mint Apple Crisp, 199
Sweet Potato Puree, 170
Sweet Potato Soup with Kale, 59

T

tamari
  Ginger Pork Chops, 103
  Spanish Chicken, 88
tapioca
  Blueberry Crinkle, 193
  Fiesta Hashbrowns, 30
Tapioca Pudding, 204
thyme
  Cajun Catfish, 153
  Honey Balsamic Chicken, 85
  Lentils with Cheese, 141
  Mediterranean Lentil Soup,
    58
  Savory Rice, 163
  Thyme and Garlic Turkey
    Breast, 81
  Thyme Roasted Sweet
    Potatoes, 167

Vegetarian Sausage and Sweet
  Pepper Hash, 30
White Bean Soup, 55
Thyme and Garlic Turkey
  Breast, 81
Thyme Roasted Sweet Potatoes,
  167
tilapia
  Lemon Pepper Tilapia, 149
tofu
  Spicy Orange Tofu, 134
tomatoes
  Artichoke-Tomato Chicken,
    83
  Chicken Chickpea Tortilla
    Soup, 46
  Hometown Spanish Rice, 162
  Honey Balsamic Chicken, 85
  Lentils with Cheese, 141
  Meat Sauce for Spaghetti, 120
  Mexi Rotini, 137
  Moroccan Spiced Stew, 63
  Pumpkin Chili, 66
  Slow-Cooker Tomato Soup, 53
  Southwestern Shredded
    Chicken, 95
  Spinach Frittata, 34
  Spinach Stuffed Tomatoes,
    131
  sun-dried
    White Beans with Sun-
      Dried Tomatoes, 171
  Sweet Potato Soup with Kale,
    59
  Unstuffed Cabbage Soup, 50
  Veggie Minestrone, 51
tomato sauce
  Baked Ziti, 138
  Greek-Style Green Beans, 182
  Meat Sauce for Spaghetti, 120
  Turkey "Spaghetti" Quinoa,
    100
tortillas
  Carnitas, 112
  Double Corn Tortilla Bake,
    135
Tropical Fruit, 200

Tropical Pork with Yams, 108
tuna
    Hot Tuna Macaroni Casserole,
      154
turkey
    breast
      Moist and Tender Turkey
        Breast, 84
      Thyme and Garlic Turkey
        Breast, 81
    ground
      Meat Sauce for Spaghetti,
        120
      Pumpkin Chili, 66
      Seven Layer Dip, 18
      Turkey "Spaghetti" Quinoa,
        100
      Unstuffed Cabbage Soup,
        50
    sausage
      Fiesta Hashbrowns, 30
      Turkey Sausage and
        Cabbage Soup, 49
Turkey Sausage and Cabbage
    Soup, 49
Turkey "Spaghetti" Quinoa, 100
turmeric
    Moroccan Spiced Stew, 63

U
Unstuffed Cabbage Soup, 50

V
Vegetarian Sausage and Sweet
    Pepper Hash, 31
Veggie Minestrone, 51

verde sauce
    Chicken Tortilla Soup, 45
vinegar
    apple cider
      Brown Sugar Pork Chops,
        105
      Tropical Pork with Yams, 108
    balsamic
      Honey Balsamic Chicken,
        85
      Slow-Cooker Beets, 175
      Spicy Beef Roast, 119
      Spicy Orange Tofu, 134
      Thyme and Garlic Turkey
        Breast, 81
    raspberry balsamic
      Raspberry Balsamic Pork
        Chops, 104
    red wine
      Artichoke-Tomato Chicken,
        83
      Spanish Chicken, 88
    rice wine
      Chicken Lettuce Wraps, 21
      Korean-Inspired BBQ
        Shredded Pork, 111

W
walnuts
    Fudgy Secret Brownies, 187
    Oatmeal Morning, 41
water chestnuts
    Chicken Lettuce Wraps, 21
White and Green Chili, 69
White Bean Soup, 55
White Beans with Sun-Dried
    Tomatoes, 171

White Chili, 67
wine
    red
      Red Wine Apple Roast, 117
Worcestershire sauce
    Gluten-Free Chex Mix, 22
    Spicy Beef Roast, 119
wraps
    Chicken Lettuce Wraps, 21

Y
yams
    Tropical Pork with Yams, 108
yeast, nutritional
    Vegetarian Sausage and Sweet
      Pepper Hash, 30
yogurt
    Greek
      Black Bean Brownies, 188
      Dates in Cardamom Coffee
        Syrup, 192
      Hungarian Beef with
        Paprika, 115
      Seven Layer Dip, 18
      Southwestern Shredded
        Chicken, 95
      White and Green Chili, 69

Z
zucchini
    Beef and Zucchini Casserole,
      123
    Chicken Dinner in a Packet,
      89
    Zucchini Chocolate Chip Bars,
      189

About the Author

Hope Comerford is a mom, wife, elementary music teacher, blogger, recipe developer, public speaker, Young Living Essential Oils essential oil enthusiast/educator, and published author. In 2013, she was diagnosed with a severe gluten intolerance and since then has spent many hours creating easy, practical, and delicious gluten-free recipes that can be enjoyed by both those who are affected by gluten and those who are not.

Growing up, Hope spent many hours in the kitchen with her Meme (grandmother) and her love for cooking grew from there. While working on her master's degree when her daughter was young, Hope turned to her slow cookers for some salvation and sanity. It was from there she began truly experimenting with recipes and quickly learned she had the ability to get a little more creative in the kitchen and develop her own recipes.

In 2010, Hope started her blog, *A Busy Mom's Slow Cooker Adventures*, to simply share the recipes she was making with her family and friends. She never imagined people all over the world would begin visiting her page and sharing her recipes with others as well. In 2013, Hope self-published her first cookbook, *Slow Cooker Recipes 10 Ingredients or Less and Gluten-Free*, and then later wrote *The Gluten-Free Slow Cooker*.

Hope became the new brand ambassador and author of Fix-It and Forget-It in mid-2016. Since then, she has brought her excitement and creativeness to the Fix-It and Forget-It brand. Through Fix-It and Forget-It, she has written *Fix-It and Forget-It Healthy One-Pot Meals Cookbook*, *Fix-It and Forget-It Slow Cooker Freezer Meals Cookbook*, *Fix-It and Forget-It Freezer to Instant Pot Cookbook*, *Welcome Home 30-Minute Meals*, *Fix-It and Forget-It Healthy Cookbook*, and many more.

Hope lives in the city of Clinton Township, Michigan, near Metro Detroit. She has been happily married to her husband and best friend, Justin, since 2008. Together they have two children, Ella and Gavin, who are her motivation, inspiration, and heart. In her spare time, Hope enjoys traveling, singing, cooking, reading books, working on wooden puzzles, spending time with friends and family, and relaxing.